Silhouettes of Life

Silhouettes of Life

Poems of Inspiration and Love

Barbara Feltquate

Copyright © 2018 by Barbara Feltquate.
Cover photograph by: Al Churilla

Library of Congress Control Number:		2018907894
ISBN:	Hardcover	978-1-9845-3880-2
	Softcover	978-1-9845-3879-6
	eBook	978-1-9845-3878-9

All rights reserved. No part of this book may be reproduced or transmitted in any form or by any means, electronic or mechanical, including photocopying, recording, or by any information storage and retrieval system, without permission in writing from the copyright owner.

The views expressed in this work are solely those of the author and do not necessarily reflect the views of the publisher, and the publisher hereby disclaims any responsibility for them.

Any people depicted in stock imagery provided by Getty Images are models, and such images are being used for illustrative purposes only.
Certain stock imagery © Getty Images.

Print information available on the last page.

Rev. date: 08/23/2018

To order additional copies of this book, contact:
Xlibris
1-888-795-4274
www.Xlibris.com
Orders@Xlibris.com
774488

Contents

Dedication xv
Prologue xvii

Chapter 1   Spiritual

When You See Through Your Heart 3
Where Is God 4
Finding Strength 5
Laughter 6
Enchanted Place 7
Principles To Live By 8
At The End Of The Day 9
Wonder In Simplicity 10
Transformation To Happiness 11
Happiness 12
People Are Just People 13
My True Friend 14
Your Inner Self 15
The Highway Of Life 16
Tranquility 17
What's The Rush? 18
The Wonders Of Your Mind 19
Think Outside The Box 20
Hands Convey Your Story 21
Is Your Head In The Clouds 22
A Child 23
A Gift From God 24
The Gift In Silence 25
Home 26

Finding Peace Of Mind 27
Through A Childs Eyes...29
The Old Tree 30

Chapter 2 <u>Lifetimes, Past, Present And Future</u>

Life Time...35
Yesterday--------Today---------Tomorrow 36
Birth Journey 37
New Born/Old Soul..38
Living Life's Journey 39
Journey To Eternity 40
Beyond Beyond-A Soul Journey 41
Lessons Of Lifetimes...42
Thoughts On Life 43
Karma Connection 44
Time...45
Your Higher Self... 46
A Young Man's Dreams… 47
Destiny's Bond...48
"The Content Of Your Characater" 49
Messages From Beyond..50
The Roaring Twenties 51
Live In The Moment...52
Devotion..53
Soulmate..54
Winters Passage 55
Setting Sun 56

Chapter 3 <u>Yoga</u>

Special Gifts..59
Namaste 60
My Teacher...61
How We Live Our Life 62
Permission To Do Nothing..63

Bored And Boring Or Upbeat And Exciting 64
Words Of Wisdom 65

Chapter 4 Love Sonnets

Circle Of Love 69
Love For Eternity 70
Cupid's Arrow 71
Will You Marry Me? 72
A Single Rose 73
A Kiss Upon My Heart 74
Love 75
Love Is In The Air 76
Bounded By Eternity 77
Love For All Seasons 78
I Remember Yesterday 79
After The Vows 80
Afterglow 82
Who Knew 83

Chapter 5 Seaside

Sunbeams 87
Moonbeams 88
Dawn 89
Daybreak At The Shore 90
Good Morning World 91
Carefree Summer Days 92
Solitary Seagull 93
The Ocean 94
Drawn To The Sea 95
Communion With The Sea 96
Dreamy Tide 97
Musical Sea 98
Musings From The Shore 99
Message From The Sea 100

Delicacies From The Sea 101
Safe Harbor 102
The Tide 103
Turbulent Tide 104
Uncharted Waters 105
Winter Landscape 106
Sunset At The Beach 107
Sunrise 108
Sunset 108
The Setting Sun 109
Endless Tides 110

Chapter 6 Sam And Ethel's Song

Ethel's Story 113
A Mother's Love 116
When Did I Become My Mother 117
Beauty 118
Making Memories 119
Memories 120
A Conversation With Mom 121
A Smile 122
It's A Gorgeous Day 124
My Interpretation 126
My Fathers Gift 127
To Mom With Love 128
The Real Person Inside 129
"I Want To Be Me!" 130
Saying Goodbye 131
A Message From Dad 132
Take My Hand 133
Together Forever 134
Remembering Mom 135
At Peace 136
You Live On 137

Chapter 7 <u>Family And Friends</u>

Toby And Rosina's Journey 141
My Unique Upbringing 143
Nonna's Sewing Table 144
To Spend A Day With You 145
A Father's Day Thank You 146
A Father's Day Issue 147
Happy Birthday Harvey-2003 148
Happy Birthday Harvey-2005 149
Happy Birthday Harvey-2017 150
In Honor Of Our 50th Wedding Anniversary 151
Celebrating 55 Years 153
My Dear Sister Janet 154
Happy 50Th Anniversary 155
Brother Lost Brother Found 156
Debbie 157
Happy 25th Wedding Anniversary Debbie And Glenn 159
A Note To Brad And Alex 160
David 161
Another Special Thank You To My Son 162
Instant Love 163
Gramps And Me 164
Ode To Ethan 166
Ethan's Poem 168
Welcome Jakob 169
Ethan And Jakob On Their Bar Mitzvahs 170
The Uniqueness Of The Day You Were Born 171
Honoring Aunt Molly 172
The In-Laws 173
Grace Ann 174
John Hanks A Talented Man 176
New Definition Of Family 177
The Gift Of Friendship 178
Friendships (Longtime or New) 179

Pamela 180
Happy Birthday Pearl... 181
Pearl's Courage 181
Sidney And Samantha.. 182
Call Me Old-Fashion 183

Chapter 8 Retirement

New Beginnings 187
Eternal Youth.. 188
Retirement... 189
Happy Retirement Harvey 190
Farewell Woburn Medical Associates 191
Thank You Woburn Medical 192
Our Journey.. 194
Reflections Of Kathy 195
Happy Retirement Cynthia 196
Gray Hair 198

Chapter 9 Travel Memories

Our Heritage 201
Our Children's Legacy 202
Images 203
A Tourists View Of New York City........................... 204
Tanglewood In The Summer 206
Beethoven's Ninth Symphony 208
Eternal Pompeii 209
A Halo Over Mt Vesuvius 210
On The Road To The Sun 211
Touch The Sky 213
Where's The Bear 214
Young Side Of Old 215

Chapter 10 Poetic Therapy

Forgiveness.. 219
Choices 220

So Speaks......A Honeydew??	221
Color Me What?	222
A Parable Between Plants And People	223
The Child Within	224
No Regrets	225
The Face In The Mirror	226
A Difficult Journey	227
Cigarette Addiction	228
Compulsive Shopper	229
Lifestyles	230
Where Is The Joy	231
A Blessed Day	232
Conquering Fear	233
Freedom To Be	234

Chapter 11 <u>In Memorium</u>

Barbara Traiger Remembered	237
The Messenger	239
Everlastng Memory	241
Friendship's Eternal Bond	242
The Essence Of You	243
Sisters Of The Soul	244
The Missing Piece Of Your Heart	245
Sue And Jill Remembered	247
The Inimitable Sue T.	249
Life As A Play	250
A Reflection	251
In Memory Of Jill Kabinoff	252
A Sunset Tribute In Memory Of Jill Kabinoff	252
Prayers And Toasts	253
A Prayer For The Traiger Family	255
A Mother's Healing Prayer	256
A Daughter's Prayer And Expression Of Gratitude	257
A Comforting Prayer	258
A Remembrance Toast	259

Chapter 12 <u>An Empowering Message</u>
    Through The Looking Glass..263
Epilogue..267
Acknowledgements..269

Also by Barbara Feltquate
Award Winning
KIDDISH YIDDISH
Jewish Traditions and Culture
in Rhyme

Dedication

'Silhouettes of Life' is dedicated to my grandchildren Brad, Alex, Ethan and Jakob in hopes that I will be giving them something tangible to remember their grandmother and the hidden gift may be to give them a better understanding of the person they are becoming or have become. I hope they find a little bit of their grandmother in themselves.

Prologue

THE WONDER OF POETRY

Poetry brings out spirituality
Poetry takes us to a place of peace
Poetry offers introspection and hope
Poetry comforts us when we grieve
Poetry enhances our celebratory joy
Poetry enables us to reveal our inner selves
Poetry is a refuge for stillness and clarity
Poetry shows a power greater than ourselves

*A poet's greatest joy is when
the reader relates and the words resonate.*

Barbara Feltquate

Chapter 1
Spiritual

When You See Through Your Heart

You view the world as God intended

Notice the joy found in simplicity
Become colorblind as skin tones blend into oneness
Celebrate the aged face lined with wisdom and beauty
Discover the softness in a hardened soul
Embrace the richness of diversity
Realize harmony on earth is a possibility

Where Is God

God surrounds us everywhere
In verdant soil and breezy air

God is the goodness in everyone
Anguished soul or wayward son

God resides deep in our heart
The merciful and forgiving part

God loves us and will dry our tears
Shouldering many of our hidden fears

God forgives and absolves our sin
Even if we are struggling within

God carries us through perilous fright
Whether turbulent storm or dark night

God vanishes prejudice and hate
Wisdom and love our crowning fate

God guides us from the moment of birth
We are His vessel for peace on earth

Finding Strength

No one travels the journey through life
Without facing problems and some strife
The more we are tested it becomes clear
We find strength we did not know was there
The enlightened among us recognize
The presence of God before our eyes
He leads us through the trouble and pain
Showing our faith and trust is not in vain
This wisdom is not easily achieved
Life's experiences go into the weave
God is the source of comforting light
A shining beacon through the night
We all share a component of God inside
Where our courage and resiliency reside
When challenges surface as they often do
God's strength is never far from you

Laughter

Laughter is like a powerful magical potion
Reducing pain and setting healing into motion

Laughter is more valuable than great wealth
Its curative powers can improve your health

Laughter can convert the meanest person
Into someone nicer and much less fearsome

Laughter can transform a stiff stern pout
Into a hilarious carefree jubilant shout

Laughter may stop hostile conflicts and war
It is hard to be angry if you giggle before

Laughter is contagious and grows rapidly
Passing it from person to person is the key

Enchanted Place

Over the hill and through the wood
A charming and enchanted cottage stood
The sun sparkled on the windowsill
The air was fragrant and very still
A pathway of flowers so beckoning
A welcome song that the birds sing
Inside vivid colors please the eye
Glistening roof tops to see the sky
The view so splendid over the bay
Not a problem stands in your way
This quiet and calming simplicity
Brings forgotten pleasures back to me
When solitude you need to find
Take this relaxing sojourn in your mind
Here in this mystical enchanted place
God puts a smile back on your face

Principles To Live By

Do not take more than your share
Give to others to show you care

Start off the day with a smile
Always go that extra mile

Be generous with a compliment
Do and say all that you meant

Show by example right from wrong
Bellow out a jubilant song

Help a child cross the street
Let a senior know they are neat

Be grateful for this beautiful day
Thanking God when you pray

At The End Of The Day

At the end of the day do you feel good
Knowing you did all that you could

At the end of the day when you look back
Are there actions you dearly wish to retract

At the end of the day do you feel content
Knowing you promised all that you meant

At the end of the day the more freely you give
Contentment surrounds the days that you live

At the end of the day can you look back with pride
Aware of God's love and presence by your side

At the end of the day if your goodness defines you
Then your purpose of life will have been true

Wonder In Simplicity

God's pure touch is in everything
From a drop of rain to bird on wing
Moonbeams dancing on the lake
The sun summoning us to wake
Bees fluttering here and there
Flowers blossoming everywhere
Viewed from the hill do you see
Luminous stars twinkling merrily
Tree tops swaying to and fro
Owls hooting soft and low
Animals protect their progeny
Cooing and fretting protectively
A mother's gentle crooning song
Soothing babe all night long
Thank You God for allowing me
To see the wonder in simplicity

Transformation To Happiness

Happiness comes from within and radiates outward
Its shiny glow touches others incandescently
Its intrinsic warmth is a source of inspiration
Transforming ever so slightly
The mundane into glimmers of sunshine
Rays of light thaw a languid core
Giving rise to optimism and hope
A pattern is established and repeated
From this intangible yet certain emotion
Begins a process of letting go to a higher being
And a discovery of inner peace
As we tap into the spark of God
That resides within
This contentment is a joyous glow
The origin of our happiness

Happiness

Happiness is not in that new shiny ring
Or wrapped package that Santa may bring
Happiness lies not in the wealth you attain
Counting your money is a lonely refrain
Happiness is the smile and glow on your face
Content and fulfilled with your purpose and place
Happiness is the musical tone in your laugh
Overcoming trying challenges put in your path
Happiness is seeing your kids mature and grow
Into adults with their young children in tow
Happiness is appreciating the simplest things
Delighting in the pleasure a new day brings
Happiness is spreading your love all around
Giving to others no greater joy can be found

People Are Just People

People are just people you realize
No matter skin or color of eyes
A rough demeanor is only a veneer
Discouraging others from coming near
People react differently to turns in life
Judge not how one deals with adversity and strife
If you look deeply into the hardest of hearts
You will find the compassionate gentle part
Self-protection is a natural guarding instinct
Trust and forgiveness are the liberating link
Removing this barrier brings our defenses down
As it starts the process of turning beliefs around
The core of your being is where God resides
Where purity and gentleness are nestled inside
This God given goodness that we all share
Will surface when we remove anxiety and fear
Imagine how uncomplicated the world could be
Adopting this forthright and simple philosophy

My True Friend

You are my best friend or worst enemy
Depending on how the mood strikes me
You oscillate between knowing it all
Or preparing yourself for a great fall
You bring me up you pull me down
You laugh at me and then you frown
You dress haute couture or lounge in sweats
The most unpredictable person I ever met
You encourage me to go out on a limb
Even if success is unsure or may be slim
You show equal measure of pride or shame
You are contritely humble or downright vain
You say others are inspired by what I do
Even when I argue your point of view
You are there for me through thick or thin
Giving me strength and courage from within
You understand and embrace my vulnerability
Because my true friend…..*YOU ARE ME!*

Your Inner Self

The person deep down inside of you
Is humbly honest and profoundly true

It is your conscience and inner guide
Where ultimate truth and wisdom reside

Your inner self is truly a faithful friend
Who will be there for you until the end

Be true to *yourself* in all that you do
And conquer the enemy if it is you

Take the kinder more modest road
Joys in life will come back ten fold

The Highway Of Life

I really enjoy a daybreak drive
Touring our beautiful country side

The road meanders here and there
Through misty morn or skies clear

The drive is like the road of life
Some with good days or with strife

If we follow a leisurely steady pace
Appreciate the grandeur of the open space

Be alert and heed the signs along the way
Our journey will be safe day after day

Tranquility

I feel at peace when I see
Something simple as a tree
It sways and sighs effortlessly
Oh how I wish it could be me

The view from the mountain
Is breathtakingly calm
It soothes and settles
Like a good healing balm

I watch a child toddle
Exploring the world
Exalting with joy
With each tiny twirl

I smell the flowers
My senses are filled
I capture the moment
The world is stilled

The sun bounces
Over the twinkling shore
I do not think
I could ask for more

Life's pleasures are simple
As you can see
When we stop and
Appreciate the tranquility

What's The Rush?

Running here
Running there
Why the race?
What happened to quiet time
To reflect and heal
To share your grace
To feel the breeze
To smell the air
To see goodness everywhere
Slow down
Breathe deeply
Feel
Listen
Hear the music in nature's symphony
Let God's palette set you free

PEACE

The Wonders Of Your Mind

A river of infinite ideas are open to find
As you unlock the potential of your mind

Allow your imagination freedom to soar high
Question the impossible and ask yourself why

Your subconscious mind is amass with creativity
While thoughts have the power to alter reality

Trust your intuition to open an untested door
There are many unlimited avenues to explore

It is easy to get caught up in routine and din
Where discord will not let new thoughts in

Set no limitations uncover every possibility
Discover the wonders of what you can see

Think Outside The Box

When you are inventive and think outside the box
You discover new vistas and remove restrictive locks

You may open a more challenging and interesting door
That an unimaginative thought process might ignore

Removing boundaries that limit what you can achieve
Opens a world of creativity some could not conceive

The greatest successes and achievements of mankind
Come from freedom of an open not constricted mind

Be unconventional not soldiers lined up one by one
Find your own rhythm and beat your own drum

Hands Convey Your Story

Hands are expressive and speak their own story
Relaying triumphs setbacks and times of glory

They communicate in a language of their own
Through gestures emotions and purpose shown

Hands joined in solemn matrimony make us one
A covenant and commitment not to be undone

A mother's hand wipes away her child's sad tear
Comforting hands wisely reassure and lessen fear

A gentle hand soothes a babe's whimpering
Curative hands calmly ease pain and suffering

A hand pumping its fist jubilantly in the air
Exalting in sweet victory held personally dear

A brandishing middle finger in an expletive stance
Message and significance delivered at first glance

Hands pampered and polished elegant and neat
Chapped and hardened toiling to make ends meet

A dramatic flair with a flamboyant wave of hand
A stopped hand raised defiantly to take a stand

Sculpting hands draw hidden depths from within
Hands in solemn prayer seek absolution of sin

Out reached hands seeking hope and healing
A thoughtful touch bestows solace and feeling

Hands leathered and knobbed respected with age
For they amass the wisdom of a scholarly sage

Is Your Head In The Clouds

There is an expression "Your head is in the clouds"
Perhaps it is an escape from the maddening crowds
Does it denote a simple and wondering mind
Or a person who is just thoughtful and kind
If you poke your head through
For a more loftier view
You ascend to a special magical place
Whose uniqueness puts a smile on your face

If your head is above the clouds …the din below is muted
If your head is above the clouds…dark clouds are below you
If your head is above the clouds…the sun glistens bright
If your head is above the clouds…vistas are unobstructed
If your head is above the clouds…you are closer to God

A Child

A child is a blessing a gift from God to you
Your role is to encourage what they can do

Show by example God's caring way
Surround them with love day after day

When they are ready to fly and test their wings
Allow them the freedom to do this pivotal thing

God will protect and guide them to their destiny
Blessing them with gifts as He did you and me

A Gift From God

The natural way you write a rhyme
Your comic flare playing the mime

Your ability to paint and sketch with ease
Charcoal and oils your creative keys

The melodic sounds that come from you
Sweeter than a nesting birds gentle coo

God loves His children unconditionally
Giving parts of Himself to you and me

Rejoice in what God has bestowed upon you
Use it wisely in all that you feel and do

The gift is grander when you readily share
Spreading His joy and love everywhere

The Gift In Silence

In silence your thoughts are the clearest and most poignant
Quietness brings on subconscious musings
Your inner voice can be heard
Listen to the messages
The ones hidden by the fray
Find your logic… your ideas… your creativity
Those thoughts that move forward in the stillness
Those precious imaginings
Where your uniqueness resides
Where beauty, grace and wonderment are untarnished
Where optimism flourishes
Mute the electronics and close your eyes
Turn off the din and let the silence speak
Give in to the music in your head…the words unsaid

Home

Home is not just an architectural thing
An extension of what money can bring

Home is not mortar or quarried stone
Or a skyscraper or cottage standing alone

Home is not a mansion with columns high
Nor a shack passed in the blink of an eye

They are simply shelters big or small
Not the substance or essential part at all

Home is where love and laughter abound
Where peace and security can be found

Home is that dwelling in your heart
The blessed contented tranquil part

Finding Peace Of Mind

In my pursuit of peace of mind
I looked and looked hoping to find

A special thing or perfect place
That would put a smile on my face

Pressures mounting day after day
So overwhelming I started to pray

I put my faith and trust in God
Letting go felt different but not so odd

Aware of His protective loving arm
I balanced my life finding no harm

The cloud blinding my eyes slowly lifted
Burdens and pressure steadily shifted

Happiness is not found in material things
Simplicity enacted the ultimate joy it brings

A restive calm flowed warmly over me
I felt peace and a sense of tranquility

I saw colorful flowers and majestic trees
Heard a soft melody in the swaying leaves

Children playfully romping in the sun
Giggling as they frolicked having fun

An elderly couple walking hand in hand
Their harmony like a jubilant band

I still have to work and pay the bills
I suffer from head colds and other ills

But I take great pleasure and delight
In doing what makes me feel right

I find contentment in family so dear
I tend to my garden and volunteer

With God alongside there is joy in my life
Knowing He will help shoulder the strife

Through A Childs Eyes

Today was so much fun and made me realize
The joys in the world through a child's eyes

A rainy day that threw your plans in a muddle
Happily accepted by a child stomping in a puddle

A child knows instantly in the blink of an eye
That clouds playfully draw pictures in the sky

That leaves swaying casually in a tree
Are whistling and humming tunes merrily

That birds frolicking lazily on the lawn
Come out to play with each new dawn

Seeing the world by removing the din
Keeps everlastingly the child within

The Old Tree

I see a gnarled and weather beaten tree
Strangely you seem to call and beckon me

What is the message you feel I must hear
Before I go through another new year

When I looked at your aged withered bark
Your branches were brittle and leaves stark

I feel that you have stood for an eternity
And your noble heart weathered valiantly

You are a symbol of honest strength and pride
You bent under pressure but you never died

Enduring the passage of time has taken its toll
Yet you proved spirit and wisdom win after all

I hear your poignant message I think you knew
Your words are simple yet uncomplicatedly true

Do not let life's seasons pass you by
Stand straight and tall and reach for the sky
Live life to its fullest be brave and kind
Share your wisdom with others
And you will enjoy peace of mind

Epilogue…after retirement as I settled into more leisurely activities and started writing more seriously and on a regular basis, my daily walk to the beach would find me passing the corner of Wianno Avenue and East

Bay Road. I was mesmerized by a very old tree. For a short while I was actually obsessed that I must see the tree daily. Finally one day the trees message became very clear. The above italicized words were actually channeled to me. I captured the trees image on film never realizing that by the end of the summer the tree would be gone…chopped down by the town Public Works department. It seems they felt it presented a potential danger if a seasonal hurricane approached. I felt sad but realized my obsession was over. The old tree had imparted its message.

Chapter 2
Lifetimes, Past, Present And Future

Life Time
A MOMENT IN ETERNITY

Savor each moment

Life is so brief

The years go by swiftly

And regrets feed our grief

Yesterday--------Today---------Tomorrow

YESTERDAY

All the remains of yesterday
Are memories and how they weigh

TODAY

Kind and insightful actions rooted in the moment
May be instrumental in future change and less atonement

TOMORROW

Is a culmination of past decisions that marked the foundation
For a fulfilling life and in God's hands a standing ovation

Birth Journey

SOARING
On wings of destiny

FLOATING
On clouds of fate

DESCENDING
Onto inviting landscape

LANDING
Into welcoming arms

DELIVERED HOME AT LAST!

New Born/Old Soul

At the moment of birth
You are the purest of heart
As you transition from your past life
To a new start

From the moment of birth
Your course is set
Your mission in life
Is to strive to perfect

It is no accident of fate
As your journey unfolds
To share your wisdom
With young and old

Instinct will guide you
Through all your days
Lessons of life times
Will shine through the maze

Love is the message
That must come through
People will be drawn
To the goodness in you

Hopefully you will attain
The ultimate goal
Of universal peace
And love on earth

…but little one for the moment
Just enjoy the rebirth

In loving memory of Lorraine (Lori) Josof

Living Life's Journey

If you live your life like a long farewell
What is important upon which to dwell

Do not look back with regret or remorse
Wishing you had followed a different course

Your legacy is not measured in what you own
But the caring fostered and love you have shown

Smile at strangers and look in their eyes
Do not be judgmental or callously criticize

See the splendor about in sight and sound
There is infinite wisdom as you gaze around

Viewing God's creation is a wonderful feeling
It is inspiring nurturing and amazingly healing

Beautiful sunrises and majestic setting sun
Count your blessings in prayer one by one

Kind thoughtful words and a helping hand
Stretches of beach and toes in the sand

Set aside quiet reflective time each day
To appreciate what has come your way

As your life journey comes to a peaceful end
Your compassion lives on with family and friend

Journey To Eternity

Climb aboard the lifetime express
Alighting or departing at any address

View your past with enlightened sighs
See the future through thoughtful eyes

The cosmic plan for all mankind
With an open mind you will find

Our goodness shines along the way
And carries us to each new day

As we follow our path to eternity
Teachings of lifetimes stay with me

At journey's end white light guides us on
To ultimate peace and an endless dawn

Beyond Beyond-A Soul Journey

Beyond beyond our journey to eternity
We aspire for perfection and serenity

Wisdom is garnered throughout the years
Experiencing joy and hope and some tears

Many separate lifetime journeys intertwine
Some paths are lost light found will shine

Sharing knowledge and goodness is the goal
With the advancement of each old soul

Enlightenment allows the freedom to soar
Rising we ascend to that celestial door

Where peace and love the world abound
A blissful rejoicing heralding sound

Dedicated to Geri Moore who spoke in
wonderment of our soul journey

Lessons Of Lifetimes

Have you ever been in a new place
As recognizable as the nose on your face
When a strong sensation of déjà vu
Settles incredibly comforting over you

Go with the impression be open to explore
You may discover you have lived before
Imagine if this concept is proven real
It explains impulses and how you feel

Allow your mind to travel back in time
Do it freely without reason or rhyme
Your intense passion of wrong or right
Might stem from injustices you had to fight

Perhaps your persistent shoulder pain
Is from a wound as a conquistador in Spain
Your natural ability to play the piano
Flashes back to when you wrote a concerto

Your first trip to Egypt down the Nile
So recognizable it brought on a smile
I could go on and on in pointing out
Past memories may remove your doubt

I have started you wondering and that is good
A process to make the implausible understood
Bringing back knowledge from far away
Enhances solving problems of the present day

If the lessons from the past are held true
The world will be better for me and you

Thoughts On Life

The purpose of life is a weighty thought
An age old question you may think about…or not

Some feel their time on the earth
Is a limited journey starting at birth

You are born, you live and then you die
As inevitable as the stars in the sky

Your legend is sustained through stories told
Memories of you fade as your friends grow old

My slant on life is a bit more philosophical
What I believe seems real and very logical

We have been here many times before
Each resurgence opens another door

Through each portal friends and loves we recognize
On a soul level not through searching eyes

The pathways we choose through eternity
Always find my love ones close to me

Together we ascend to that ultimate place
Of love and peace for the whole human race

Karma Connection

Our soul meeting was not an accident of fate
A lesson was imparted on that time and date
There was unfinished work from my life past
Ready to be fulfilled with knowledge amassed
Our conversations were deeply enlightening
My sojourn to a past life a little frightening
Your words and lesson etched in my memory
Their wisdom and truth now a vital part of me
Our crossing pathway was timely but fleeting
Our souls will connect again at a future meeting
You confirmed my very strong conviction
That on soul level we find our connection
In this life time or next we will meet again
We are eternally connected my soul friend

Epilogue:

I write of my friend, Geri Moore. Our paths crossed for a short period time. She moved away and shortly thereafter passed away. Her words still reverberate in my head and heart. I am sure she would be pleased that I still tap into my hidden creativity.

Time

The concept of time is intriguing to me
Is it one dimensional or tiered indefinitely

Is the moment lived, passed and gone
Or is there a continuum that carries along

Does breaking a time barrier allow us to be
In ancient Rome one day then another galaxy

Can we pass into a portal by wishing it true
Or must we depend on science to carry us through

Is it some miracle of faith or strong magical potion
That past and future journeys are set into motion

Time passes so quickly is lamented quite frequently
I believe there are many lifetimes to enjoy leisurely

Your Higher Self

Your higher self the purest part of you
Embodies love and wisdom in all you do

From the time of birth as we grow old
Our distinctive personalities will unfold

We journey through experiences of life
Identified as daughter mother or wife

As we begin to pursue our spirituality
We focus on the path of our destiny

Seeking the truth and sense of who we are
Beyond the eyes and the furthest star

We are lead to a state of enlightenment
Hearing the voice of love as He meant

Attaining one with the Godliness in you
The ultimate aspect of your being is true

A Young Man's Dreams...

...AN OLD MAN'S MEMORIES

I AM GOING TO FIND A BEAUTIFUL WOMAN!

*I learned the meaning of love and shared life's
Joys walking hand in hand with my beloved wife*

I AM GOING TO HAVE A DOZEN CHILDREN

*I was blessed with a daughter and a son
A treasured gift and a source of forgivable pride*

I AM GONG TO BE THE BOSS!

*I toiled well, gave an honest day's labor
And earned the respect of my fellow workers*

I AM GOING TO CLIMB THAT MOUTNTAIN

*I weathered the storms and met life head on
I felt God's presence and was unafraid along the way*

I AM GOING TO CONQUER THE WORLD!

*I accepted my limitations and made the most of my strengths.
I did my best and with no regrets I can rest content*

Destiny's Bond

Did we meet before
At some distant shore
In a time long passed
A lifetime gone
A memory stirs
A feeling so strong
Your name is unknown
But my heart is at home
We are walking closer
Do you feel the draw
Am I alone in this need
To touch and explore
To melt in your arms
And know peace once more
When past loves reunite
The circle is complete
Destiny's bond

"The Content Of Your Characater"

An interpretation of the quote by Heraclitus
(540-480BC) a Greek Philosopher

The content of your character is *your* choice
How you think and perform in action or voice
Each day what you say, choose, or action you do
Gives rise to the person who evolves into you
Change is the constant in life's great plan
It tests the resilience and strength of man
Facing the challenges that life presents
Tolerance and grace are your defense
Your honor guides the light of your sum
As you evolve into what you will become
With kindness forgiveness and integrity
Your character will forge your destiny

Messages From Beyond

Supernatural!
Believe…or not!
Preoccupied with
Dreams or thought?

Spirit world energy does exist
Guiding through the shadowy mist
Surrounding us in protective light
Steering us to do what is right
Sheltering through the darkest storm
Circling protection with each new morn
Go with your instinct it will be true
Follow the messages being sent to you
Think of it as a powerful magical wand
Directing and guiding from beyond
Till we meet again on the other side
Watch for telltale signals far and wide

The Roaring Twenties

The roaring twenties was a time of unusual frivolity
Indulging in extreme life styles without apology
The Flapper defined the country's fashion and song
In short skirts and bobbed hair dancing all night long
There was a rejection of morals and denial of prohibition
Disregarding long standing decorum and tradition
The movement brought on an era of change and some equity
That altered women's submissive culture and improved their destiny
This evolution was a push to ban together to promote
Gender equality obtaining the right to vote
The free spirited craze did not survive the great depression
But… lead to the dawn of woman's freedom of expression

Live In The Moment

Yesterday is gone it is memory
Tomorrow will be your destiny
Today is a gift of the present

Be mindful of the treasure of each day
Live it thoughtfully in a loving way
Store it as a joyous part of your legacy
Anticipating the blessings of what's to be

Devotion

~A SOUL JOURNEY~
Dedicated to the memory of Charlotte and Uncle John

As we have travelled time through eternity
Your loving and devoted spirit will find me
Recognition is perpetually swift and sure
Our souls resonate comfortably as before

In this lifetime we are uncle and niece
Discovering instant happiness and peace
There to support and protect each other
As loyal friend, family, sister or brother

Our relationship is spiritual in its depth
Safeguarded and upheld to our last breath
With a commitment profound and strong
Dedicated to preserve and guide along

Taking pride and joy in what is achieved
Never hampered by life's tangled weave
When weakened both feel the pain
Guardsmen against wind and rain

Reassuring through gladness and sorrow
Powerfully united as we face tomorrow
As each resurgence commences anew
Our guiding lights will follow through

There to welcome at portals door
Then send you off and watch you soar
Our spiritual connection will be found
Time and place hold no bound

Soulmate

When one believes strongly in life's continuity
I look at you at a soul level and can plainly see

Our lives have touched numerous time before
We have assisted each other opening many a door

It was not randomness nor accident of time or fate
When my dear son David chose you as his mate

We have had a strong connection through eternity
As friend, sister or mother with babe at knee

We are old souls with wisdom and lessons to share
We guide and lovingly nurture those we hold dear

Wishing you happy birthday dear soulmate of mine
As I will and have through many lives over time

Epilogue:

Anne and David will be celebrating their 20th anniversary on October 24, 2018. Anne and I appreciate and honor our special relationship as soulmates do.

Winters Passage

Winter's heralded landscape
Fading in the light
Shadows in the sunset
Merging with the night
Echoes of a lifetime
Whisper in the wind
Season's gallant salute
Before the lights are dimmed
Winter yields to the golden arc
Enhanced in a brilliant infernal
Heavenly peace renewal rebirth
Spring hopes eternal

Setting Sun

Oh setting sun
I view you with wonder and hope
I am mesmerized by your brilliance
The most magnificent sight to behold
A golden sphere that dominates the sky
You melt into the horizon vibrant and bold
You are steadfast in your mission
Your poignant message is clear

*"Journey's end does not designate the end of things
A new day will follow with the hope it brings
Life cycles renew our faith and the power of God's majesty
Each new dawn brings us closer to our own destiny"*

Chapter 3
Yoga

Special Gifts

Thank you for sharing your special gifts
Bringing on light and lifting the mist
You live your life in a kind gentle way
With inner peace you welcome each new day
You remind us perfection is not our goal
The journey is what nourishes and fills our soul
You help us find our calming breathe and realize
The magnificence of nature before our eyes
Appreciate the splendor of the rising sun
Knowing God and the universe are truly one

Dedicated to Lauren Vines, my yoga instructor extraordinaire, whose classes and inspiring readings have influenced me greatly in my search for inner peace

Namaste

A Buddhist greeting started long ago
Expressing our oneness without ego
In prayer fashion is how we start
Bringing hands to center heart
Bow your head and close your eyes
Chant OHMMMMM in gentle sighs
A timeless bond of spirituality
Joins the sweetness in you to me
We honor those we have not met
Treat those close by with respect
Love will guide us along the way
May peace be with you all the day

Om Shanti, Shanti, Shanti
Peace Peace Peace
Namaste

My Teacher

My teacher is the one who opened my eyes
To explore vistas in wondrous surprise

My teacher prompted me to delve inside
Where my center of being in serenity resides

My teacher explained there is no basis for fear
When anxieties and doubts are menacingly near

My teacher inspired setting myself free
Uncovering the amazing woman within me

My teacher advised to your own self be true
Then wisdom and knowledge will follow you

My teacher taught me awareness has no end
Thank you for being my teacher and good friend

Dedicated to Lori Josof who opened my eyes to explore all possibilities and whose friendship and wisdom I will always remember

How We Live Our Life

"Live your life as you wish the world to be"
The wise Yogi's words resonate with me

For every selfless and caring act we do
The ramifications will surely accrue

Creating a world filled with harmony and peace
Where man's inhumanity to man may cease

Wars would be a thing of the past
Hunger and indifference would not last

Forgiveness purges the soul of anger and hate
An act of compassion is never too late

Encourage and share with those in need
Show gratitude in action and deed

Smile warmly rather than wear a frown
Lift your head up instead of down

Laughter is joyous and eases a cry
Say hello to friendship and not good bye

Kindness paid forward is a universal plan
That could bring peace throughout the land

Permission To Do Nothing

If pressures and stress day in and day out
Are so consuming you have the urge to shout

When you feel your sanity and spirit are at stake
Give yourself permission to take a needed break

Remove yourself mentally from draining tension
Find a quiet state of mind to focus your attention

Ignore the tug of quilt trying to pull you back
Try this form of mindfulness to keep on track

Take a moment to enjoy the stillness of the day
Appreciate a flower or puffy cloud drifting away

Think of daybreak or sunset so peaceful and still
Remember these quiet moments are yours at will

Your mind can bring you to a tranquil state
A calming approach whose benefits are great

When it is time for you to get back in the race
This approach to life's demands can slow the pace

A meditative break removing yourself from the din
Is a wonderful way to restore your balance within

It is okay....
Give yourself permission to do nothing!

Bored And Boring
Or
Upbeat And Exciting

Each day is a treasured gift presented to you
Why would you complain there is nothing to do
If boredom and reproach make up your day
You might want to rethink your ho-hum way
Upbeat people are usually in a good mood
Openly social displaying a positive attitude
People are drawn to a cheerful beaming face
A dower expression takes you out of the race
Make an effort to greet the new day with fun
Be happy and count your blessings one by one
Some feed off those who are exuberantly outrageous
Their antics spread like a ailment that is contagious
If you are loud with nothing constructive to say
It is never too late to change your lackluster way
Repeat "life is good" "life is good" in mantra style
I choose to be upbeat and share my glowing smile
There is a choice it is simple and quite clear
Do not waste a lifetime that should be held dear

Your choice!

Inspired by Lauren Vines, my Yoga teacher, who exudes warmth, is nonjudgmental, and spreads sunshine as she greets each day as a treasured gift

Words Of Wisdom

"Life is a vessel with boundless capacity
Restored by natures magnificent audacity"

These words of wisdom were given to me
I treasure them for their timeless simplicity

We have the ability to replenish our reservoir
By meditating on the furthest imaginative star

Your heart center should be the calming place
Where you find your rhythm and set your pace

Greet each day as the glorious sun rises high
Enjoy the drifting clouds and bright blue sky

Hear the symphony in nature's sweet sound
Whirling wind or patter of rain on the ground

Feel the sun's warmth shining down on you
It is the inspiring guide in all that we do

Saluting the landscape refocuses our reverie
Bringing forth insight and openness for discovery

Rejoicing in God's bounty an idyllic way to start
Revitalizing the peace and love in our heart

Chapter 4
Love Sonnets

Circle Of Love

Lost love
Hearts searching

Found love
Hearts reuniting

Old love
Hearts in harmony

Eternal love
Hearts at peace

Love abound
Every time around

Love For Eternity

My love for you has no end
Destiny dictates that we spend
Lifetimes in rapturous sweet embrace
Pleasure and pain together face

Each resurgence is incomplete
Until souls in recognition meet
Peace and joy and hope are found
In love eternal we are bound

To fly away on joyous wings
Knowing that our love will bring
Us together through eternity
Until we can no longer be

Cupid's Arrow

Cupid's arrow finds its mark when least expected
Dizzy as a bleating lark resistance is affected

Age is not a barrier nor time nor place or season
Struck by the unseen carrier a piercing beyond reason

Silly laughs and broad grin smile rational thought evasive
Neither craft nor hidden guile a look so persuasive

Floating on wings of love light hearted and carefree
Soaring through clouds high above enjoy your destiny

Cupid-Classical Mythology
God of desire, erotic love, affection and attraction

Will You Marry Me?

This question has been asked on bended knee
Up on an airplane or down in the sea

While parachuting buoyantly through the air
Or on a Ferris wheel at the county fair

As an impromptu suggestion on the Vegas strip
Or on the Alpine slope before a clumsy slip

With a ring hidden in freshly made cobbler pie
Coughed down with an astonished gulping sigh

While being wheeled into the delivery room
By the frantic daddy who soon will be the groom

Whether traditional or in avant-garde style
You are the only one to bring on my smile

I love you and want you for my wife
Please say yes so we can start our life

A Single Rose

A single rose signifies
A simple and pure love
Its fragrance lingers
Pleasantly in the air above
The thorns are a reminder
That some days will see some pain
Along with the sunshine
There will be a little rain
The soft red petals
So silky to the touch
Say to you only
I love you very much

A Kiss Upon My Heart

A kiss upon my heart
A most romantic gesture
Knowing from the start
Our love is beyond measure
A treatise to your devotion
Your sonnet humble and sweet
Fills my world with emotion
A kiss that skips a beat
Splendor in your touch so right
With reverence and hesitation
Transcends darkness into light
In caressing trepidation
The pulse of our longing
All other desires at rest
Your seed in the morning
Suckled at my breast

Love

The ramifications of love are amazing
The warmth it exudes radiates within
and without

Its invisible glow has the ability to touch not
only that place deep in your core but warm
the hearts of those around you

It overshadows darkness and brings hope
It promotes dreams and the realization that
nothing is impossible

Love is so powerful
It is stronger than any man-made force
Love is the most potent weapon of mankind
…and brings you the closest to God

Love Is In The Air

Springtime love in the air
Sweetness felt everywhere

Air so fragrant senses fill
Capture moments at your will

Musical melody swaying motion
Feel laughter's sweet emotion

Butterflies flutter to each flower
Spreading magic by the hour

Sunbeams dance on the sea
Glittering essence surrounds me

Share this wonder in what you do
From the hilltop shout

"I LOVE YOU"

Bounded By Eternity

Each romantic gesture
Brings me closer to you
Like the rose on my pillow
Kissed with morning dew

Your eyes sparkle in wonder
As you gaze lovingly at me
The vision makes us ponder
Loves inevitability

Hand in hand together
Pulses beating musically
Knowing we are forever
Bounded by eternity

Love For All Seasons

Spring time love burns so intense
Burgeoning rapture no defense
Blood pulsates at passions peak
Bold and firm and rosy cheeked

Summer time with lazy days
Stealing hours to run and play
Idle frolic over hill and dale
The dance of love will prevail

Autumn passion sweet and slow
Romance brings on a hidden glow
Hearts entwined in fulfilling embrace
A contented smile plays upon your face

Winter's chill is in the air
Eyes behold beauty fair
Beloved come warm my heart
As you did from the start

I Remember Yesterday

I remember yesterday
As if it were today
The energy and excitement
Young lovers at play
Every feeling fresh
Each sweet embrace
Sent me a tremble
A glow upon my face

I remember yesterday
As if it were today
A babe in my arms
To guide along the way
Each eager step a blessing
Turn and you were grown
Flying on ardent wings
Never forgetting home

I remember yesterday
As if it were today
Settled in our golden years
Gratefully I pray
Life is a kaleidoscope
Colors and shapes anew
Thank you for my memories
Each day was a gift from You

After The Vows

In my dreams I saw us
The alter of stars above
Our hands joined and starry eyed
We declared our eternal love

It was the moment all girls live for
From toddler to maidenhood
Hopes and dreams united
Happily after understood

I woke from my dreamy slumber
And shook my groggy head
My reverie was short lived
It was forty years later instead

Gone was my filmy night gown
A faded flannel in its place
Springy brunette locks were gray now
And matted to my face

What is that grating sound
A rumbling and a roaring
Prince Charming's still asleep
Honking and snoring

Standing in front of the mirror
Turning from side to side
When did my chest fall
And my hips get so wide

Are those more gray hairs
And another wrinkle or two
Better get a move on
Before I get too blue

Hubby is a stirring
On the other side of the bed
He is still so very handsome
As he yawns and scratches his head

He looks at me in that sweet way
I know he wants to tarry
At that moment I realize
He sees the girl he married

What does not seem to change
As we grow old together
The eyes only see
The love for one another

Afterglow

Who ever thought after so many years
Of mortgages schedules and wiping away tears

Of nurturing children and watching them grow
We would enjoy such pleasure in life's afterglow

That special warmth that spreads from within
As husband and wife find passion again

Not quite like the excitement of days gone by
With splashes of color that radiate the sky

But like the steadfastness of the setting sun
Our lives are fulfilled because we are one

Who Knew

Who knew...
The sky was so vividly blue

Who knew...
The wind whispered a soft gentle tune

Who knew...
The birds sang a sweet soothing song

Who knew...
A smile could melt an unsuspecting heart

Who knew...
The raptures of youth could be rekindled

Who knew...
Love could blossom anew

Who knew...
All dreams could come true

*Inspired by an acquaintance who surfaced from a difficult divorce and her amazement when unexpectedly and without any expectations she met a gentleman who changed the course of her life....
Her exclamation of "Who knew!" stuck with me.*

Chapter 5
Seaside

Sunbeams

Did you ever watch a sunbeam
Spread its wings of gold
Dance upon the waters
Our universe enfold

Those golden eyelets
Lighten our despair
Put a smile upon our lips
Wash away our fear

Even through the darkest
Rain trodden day
High above the heavy clouds
The sunbeams are at play

There is something spiritual
A message in each ray
They are God's reminder to
Rejoice in the day

Moonbeams

Did you ever watch a moonbeam
Glow in the sky above
Sail across the heaven
Like a graceful dove

Those radiant rays shield peril
From the somberness of night
Giving us peace and comfort
Casting off our fright

Even when the sparkle
Cannot be seen
Its brilliance still rejoices
On a celestial beam

There is great comfort
Whether night or day
Knowing God's presence
Guides us all the way

Dawn

With the dawn of each new day
Endless possibilities come my way

New beginnings lay at my door
Countless wonders to explore

Each ray projects a shiny beam
A glorious ride to fulfill a dream

Daybreak gives way to hope anew
The joys in life lay in front of you

Daybreak At The Shore

Eagerly awaiting the suns glorious glow
A perfect time and place to relax and let go

Excitement mounting in expectant delight
In wonder and awe to behold a grand sight

The morning sun rises in welcoming splendor
Remnants of the night in reluctant surrender

Incoming tide reassuringly kisses the shore
While the ascending sun opens a mystical door

Breezes can be heard through the tall grass
Softly chanting good morning to all who pass

The miracle and magic as night turns into day
Brings hope and expectation along the way

Good Morning World

Good morning world how do you do
The sun is shining the sky is blue

People passing smile and nod hello
Flowers and colors wherever you go

Birds soar high and effortlessly
Peace and quiet settles over me

Beauty of nature the world adorn
God has given us this beautiful morn

Carefree Summer Days

I open my sleepy eyes and say
It is going to be a beautiful day

The sky so blue…the trees so green
The prettiest back drop ever seen

Springing from my comfy bed
I ponder what events lay ahead

So many pathways I can choose
Structure my day or just hang loose

Placing my hands firmly on my hips
A mischievous smile upon my lips

Chores and duties can wait another day
I decide it would be amusing to play

Solitary Seagull

Oh lonely seagull perched on your post
Guarding the harbor and acting as host

You proudly gaze over the ocean tides
Nothing is lost by your searching eyes

The sun over the horizon declares it is day
Your wings flutter in an expectant way

You cockle and shrill at the other gulls
In a language understood by nobody else

Flying near the mast of an arriving boat
You watch it bob and yawl to stay afloat

The sky is blue with a teasing of haze
Forecasting a harbinger of sunny days

While the surf pounds the sandy shore
You guard your domain forever more

The Ocean

The lure of the ocean for me is great
Affording peaceful moments to contemplate

When this fascination started is hard to say
But it gives me pleasure day after day

The pleasing sounds and sights hypnotize
God's glorious splendor is before my eyes

I observe the horizon melting into the sea
With the grace and timelessness of eternity

The rainbow pallet at sunset holds me bound
A brilliant dazzle nowhere else to be found

The morning sun shimmering on for miles
Makes me believe God looks down and smiles

Drawn To The Sea

Drawn to the sea for no particular reason
Day or night, night or day at any season

The way the sun glows and sparkles down
Brings on a smile and removes a frown

The hypnotic and steady lapping of the sea
Is a calming balm and restorative to me

The steadfastness of each new tide
Reminds me God is always by my side

Communion With The Sea

Idle ambling brings me to the shore
Drawn by sounds and something more

Surely it is not happenstance
That brought me to nature's dance

Of sea and sky and birds aloft
Breezes gentle and so soft

Misty morn fades into glowing sun
Dew drops sparkle all in fun

Sea grass sways with grace and ease
Whispering winds hug the silky sleeves

Squawking gulls gliding over head
Protecting the harbor it could be said

The magic in nature's show
Fills my senses to overflow

My cup refilled a day of rebirth
From this special place on earth

Thank you God for giving me
My communion with the sea

Dreamy Tide

Strolling each day to the beckoning beach
Discovering God's bounty within my reach

The water is low at the rocky shore
Exciting new treasures lay at tides door

The ocean's edge seems so far away
Shimmering sands feel the suns ray

View a scattering of seaweed and rocks
Driftwood from exotic far away docks

Imagination free to ramble and roam
Taking me to places far from home

Behold puddles that are shiny and glisten
Hear them speak if you patiently listen

Look! Yonder! A Viking long ship
Alas it vanishes with each ocean dip

Conjure the majesty of the parting sea
It happened for Moses why not me?

Mermaids twirling under the sun
Sea horses prancing one by one

Time to leave as nature does it thing
Ocean waters wash away what they bring

What does not change or fade away
Freedom to dream and rejoice in the day

Musical Sea

The oceans rhythm is music to my ears
Inspiring hope and washing away tears

The ebb and flow of the enduring sea
Reminds me of a wondrous symphony

The cadence of the waves on the shore
Perform a philharmonic musical score

The crescendo builds to its ultimate high
Symbols clash and drums echo by

When the tide slowly pulls away
The tinkle of the ivories are at play

The magic and lore in the sea is found
When *you* hear its melodious sound

Musings From The Shore

There is nothing as calming and beautiful I say
Then the sun rising over water starting a new day

Ocean birds chirping in their own tongue
Announcing to the universe the day has begun

The tides gentle motion has a comforting beat
Its hypnotic lulling rhythm a special treat

I spot large fluffy clouds here and there
A soft gentle breeze and they disappear

There on the horizon so infinitely small
A vessel is sighted no larger than a ball

I can sit here for hours in this special place
Away from the crowds and inevitable race

Viewed from this rocky and sandy shoal
I feel serenity and harmony deep in my soul

Peace and contentment each day a rebirth
From this special watery place on the earth

Message From The Sea

I am not conveying tales of mystical lore
Of a bobbing bottle or one on the ocean floor
Nor a message written and sent to its destiny
Fortuitously found by sailor wondering the sea
It is not Charles Dickens long ago classic book
Which in hindsight gives pause for a second look
I refer to the sounds of the oceans ebb and flow
Rhythmic pulses that speak more than you know
Close down your senses use inner searching eyes
The cadence is seductive and will mesmerize
The soothing sound of the waves reduces stress
Teaches us calmness and open mindedness
Whether pounding surf or gentle humming
A soft easy tide or powerful drumming
The message echoed over the din is clear
God's steadfastness is always there

Delicacies From The Sea

I salivate and my palate is alert
Not for meat or decadent dessert
But for unusual savory delicacies
Especially if they live on the seas
One of my favorite foods is squid
I had my first taste as a kid
A sea urchin's prickly skin
Holds a treasure trove within
Oysters are credited in love lore
Give me a dozen….or more
The trawling crab must not forget
The ever overhead looming fishing net
Succulent lobster meat dripping in butter
Its appearance before made me shudder
Periwinkles in the crawling snail family
Steamed with garlic a tempting delicacy
Whinnying sea horses gallop by
Starfish reflected in the sky
The tides bring in each new day
A gastronomical treat your way

Safe Harbor

The harbor is a quaint picturesque place
Where grand boats and small sails vie for space

Quiet fishing boats armed with rods and reels
Share the channel with echoing laughter and peals

Protected from the ravages of the high sea
Boats bob with grace dreamy and carefree

Follow your fantasies be open to explore
New adventures lay at each distant shore

When your needs are filled and satisfied
Chart your course with the incoming tide

Back to nature's secure protective arm
Anchored and feeling safe from harm

Safe harbor is what God has given me
A place where I challenge my creativity

He taught me not trying is a greater sin
Denying myself the hidden riches within

I conquered my dire anxiety and fear
Knowing safe harbor and God is near

He enabled me to explore the vast unknown
Knowing there is a special place called home

The Tide

The ebb and flow of the ocean tide
Gives me great comfort deep inside

Through angry gale or placid sea
Its steadfastness encourages me

Oceans replicate life in many ways
Turbulence is followed by calming days

As the sun creates a shimmering shoal
Absorb its strength as a future goal

The seas rhythm as it meets the shore
Reinforces our faith and opens a door

Weather the storms that come along
Knowing nature's balance is very strong

Each tide brings a brand new day
God in his wisdom made it that way

Turbulent Tide

Out of nowhere rough waters arise
Taking you completely by surprise

A turbulent storm on the high sea
Tosses and turns you mercilessly

Dark and foreboding clouds ahead
A tempest is brewing viewed with dread

Stand the course hold on tight
Faith will carry you through the night

The sun rises bright and clear
Life so precious is still there

Trust in God to guide you through
Treasure life and each day anew

Uncharted Waters

When I allow myself to look within
Beyond confusion and away from the din

In that place in my heart of heart
Where peace and happiness really start

I separate from the demands to succeed
The more you have the more you need

Once you take that fateful leap
And experience feelings that run deep

Pressures and stress will fade away
As the beauty around you fills your day

Your world will be simplified
No superficial needs or false pride

Your senses will be filled to overflow
Submerged in love and an inner glow

The intrinsic value of life is clear
You will recognize what to hold dear

Winter Landscape

I came upon a dramatic crystalline scene
A vision more spectacular than any dream

A sea shore landscape on a sunny winter day
Its stark splendor nearly carried me away

The glistening sun gave a spectacular show
Ice crystals like diamonds sparkled aglow

Glacial cubes drifting along the ocean edge
Stacked randomly creating a scenic ledge

Ducks floated by on the glassy surf
Shore birds guarded their frigid turf

I captured this moment in my memory
Nature showed a glimpse of her majesty

Sunset At The Beach

Slapping waves churning
Distant gulls piercing squawk
Chattering......Gathering
A steady procession
A pilgrimage old as time
Drawn to the daily ritual
Spirit Suns tribute to Mother Earth
Settle on sandy turf, piling or protruding jetty
Seek your vantage point
Through silky sea grass or hardy rugosa
Fiery striations of gold spread exalted arms
Paying homage to day and welcoming night
Inspiring... Equalizing... Inevitable...
Descent to Destiny
Silence... Tangible awe... Breathless anticipation
Sizzle... Ahhh
Ultimate moment unity and peace

Sunset at the Beach

Sunrise

Open your eyes
Behold a beautiful day
What great adventures
Lay before me I say
I can scale a mountain or
Dance on the shore
Fly over the tree tops
And search for more
I flex my muscle
Stretch and shout
Watch me world
I am coming out!

Sunset

Close my eyes
Rejoice in the day
Mission accomplished
I proudly say
I rose and soared
Enjoyed the view
I played and toiled
Helped mankind too
I rest at peace
I did all that I could
I burst with joy
When you say-I did good

The Setting Sun

Oh setting sun viewed with wonder and hope
You valiantly descend on your downward slope

You melt into the horizon bright and bold
The most magnificent sight to behold

Your poignant message is loud and clear
Pursue your destiny without any fear

In your quiet and majestic way
You rise anew day after day

Endless Tides

I am at peace when I see
The ocean tides open and free

A blending of horizon and blue sky
A majestic wonder fills the eye

Its steadfastness conveys to me
The symbolic travel to our destiny

Each day brings in a challenge new
Testing our stamina as we plow through

Receding water wash difficulties away
The incoming tide brings in a new day

Chapter 6
Sam And Ethel's Song

Ethel's Story

Born in Boston on November fifth nineteen twenty-one
The year Rudolph Valentino's "the Sheik" made its run
Brother Nathan was seven and born in the old country
   Five years later sister Molly would join the family
Ethel lived on Bullfinch and then a street called Lynde
   So many cultures and nationalities you could find
     She was thought of as a loner yet daring kid
       Inquisitive adventurous and free spirited
     She triumphantly sledded down Frog Pond Hill
     Or boldly road a rented bicycle without a spill
     She jumped hydrants playing the tomboy role
And shimmied exuberantly down the fireman's pole
   Her picture in the Herald American is family lore
     Featuring the stylish pajama pants that she wore
     It brought her a marriage proposal in the mail
     Today the perverse sender would end up in jail
     In 1938 she graduated from Girls High School
Winning the coveted Palmer writing prize-how cool
A mishap at NY's World's Fair almost altered her fate
  Saved by Bubbe and Aunt Mima before it was too late
     She first saw "Sammy" at Lazaro's ice cream store
      He was so handsome as he walked past the door
    There was a romantic attraction from the start
      And his protective attention won her heart
      Like Lancelot he rescued her at the dance
     From then on no other suitor had a chance
They swayed to the collegiate shag all night long
As he whispered in her ear and sang a sweet song
     They dated and wooed secretly for a year or so
     Not wanting their interfaith families to know
     True love and romance conquers all in the end
      Their tender relationship was a perfect blend

Their marriage caused many tongues to wag
At times it was hurtful and a terrible drag
They moved to Myrtle Street where I was born
During a record breaking winter ice storm
My earliest and fondest childhood memory
Is the ghetto on Blue Hill Ave in Roxbury
So many hand me downs and baby carriages
Ice cream wagon chimes love and marriage
Mom with gingham apron and spatula in hand
Concocting tantalizing meals to beat the band
The delightful aromas that wafted in the air
Drawing in residents and family far and near
She looked so chic dressed for a party or play
In her Persian lamb coat and matching beret
We owned the streets first black and white TV
Neighbors watched from our porch with curiosity
Zayde wanted to secure some prime real estate
Partnering with son-in-law Sam as his work mate
Fate intervened and the plan did not come to fruition
The dream of building a house became our new mission
Soon we had grown into an active family of five
When cute little Janet and then Larry arrived
Mom and Dad decided to construct their own home
At four thousand five hundred no need for a loan
Dad put us all to work pitching in on this endeavor
The project became an ordeal and seemed to last forever
Time marches on the kids married and moved away
Letting mom and dad think about recreation and play
They now had grandchildren numbering six
Soon 11 great-grandchildren would add to the mix
They moved to Florida on the states east coast
For fun and foolishness they used to boast
Working backstage on Dad's "Little Show"
Ethel was the silent support that made it a 'go'
Dad sadly has been gone for many a year

Mom dealt admirably with loneliness and fear
As her positive and upbeat attitude arose once more
It is her legacy and legend that we admire and adore
Quite vocal and passionate about her political stand
An avid and frequent CNN watcher on broadband
She loves old movie films and romantic books
Still has retained her extraordinary good looks
Family and friends enjoy being in her company
She approaches ninety with a smile and dignity
We have assembled adoringly from far and wide
Forming a circle of love and devotion side by side
Dearest Mom, we honor and pay homage to you
Love and wisdom is reflected in all the you do

Epilogue:

*I read this poem to Mom at her 90th birthday party.
She loved it and proclaimed it was amazingly accurate.*

A Mother's Love

From the moment your eyes opened and gazed into mine
A bond forged between us so easy to define
Your wellbeing was placed in my loving care
A promise I accepted until I am no longer here
You were a treasure I cherished from the start
Your hand clenched my finger and tugged at my heart
The need to protect you so overwhelmingly strong
It grew with intensity as the years moved along
I worried and fretted as all mother's do
Wisely balanced with knowing I must not smother you
You are all grown up now and doing just fine
Still my love and protection defy distance and time
No matter you age or status or strife
A Mother's love is forever
A child is for life

Dedicated with love and devotion
to my mother Ethel Amato

When Did I Become My Mother

It was not that many years ago
As a child my mother had me in tow

I followed her to the local merchant shop
Watching her barter always staying on top

Waves of mortification would wash over me
As she negotiated a price reducing the fee

Years later around the conference table I sit
Brokering a business deal using all of my wit

My colleagues praise my extraordinary acuity
I credit mother whose skills passed down to me

Beauty

Beauty to me has nothing to do
With flawless skin and eyes of blue

Clothes do not the person make
Judging by wealth a tragic mistake

Couturier fashion dripping in jewels
An arrogant smile has nobody fooled

Beauty radiates from within your soul
Humility and kindness embody the whole

A compassionate and benevolent heart
Measures magnificence from the start

Your selfless caring and elegant grace
Reflects the genuine beauty of your face

Making Memories

Mom, Janet and I went on an adventurous cruise
Leaving behind routines, challenges and daily news

Appreciating the tranquility bobbing across the seas
Relaxation and fun replace stress in the ocean breeze

We chuckled at our quarters so compact and neat
Not bumping each other was an extraordinary feat

Appreciating the ships setting its splendor and luster
Struggling with life jackets we almost failed muster

We made new friends and introduced each other
Proudly proclaiming this is our cherished mother

A nightly promenade after gaming at the slots
A small dramine pill for queasy stomach knots

We dined watched shows laughed and reminisced
Ending each night with thanks and a grateful kiss

We thanked God for giving us another perfect day
Its joy and contentment would carry us a long way

The future is thought of warily but without regret
We made a precious memory we will never forget

Our first Caribbean cruise together…mother and her daughters…
She walked around beaming and so did we.

Memories

Special Moments Remembered

Dearest our life was like a storybook
In twilight it pleases me to take a look

Recalling events indelible in my mind
To retrieve later when serenity to find

As simple as that radiant summer sunset
Or the strong feelings on the day we met

Month after month and year after year
Those things I wish to always hold dear

In the winter and solemn days of my life
As I struggle with aging and strife

Like the pages of a masters great book
Our life fans before me to take a look

I am content and find true peace
Reliving those moments that never cease

This poem was prompted by a conversation with my mother, Ethel, a few months before she passed away when she exclaimed ever so earnestly, "Isn't life just like a book"

A Conversation With Mom

Barbara: "Mom, what are you thinking about?"….
(In reference to life and though unspoken….her decline)

Mom: "One never knows what the next hour will bring"

"Appreciate time and enjoy the moment"

"Beautiful memories bring peace"

"Have I told you lately that I love you?"

My mother, Ethel, was an amazing woman who personified wisdom and love. She left a wonderful and meaningful legacy.

A Smile

You meet the nicest people
Everywhere you go
Did you ever stop and notice
They respond to your special glow

Why is it that you never
Encounter harbingers of gloom
Because your infectious smile
Brings out their inner bloom

It takes so little energy
To conquer and to win
To transform a frown
Into a toothy grin

You start a chain reaction
Whose momentum is unknown
As it dramatically develops
Exponentially a life of its own

Each of your brief encounters
Pass on an individual ray
On and on people connect
In a very special way

The secret is so simple
To brighten up each day
No potions or hidden vials
Just open up and give out

A GREAT BIG SMILE

*Inspired by loving memories of my father,
Sam Amato*

It's A Gorgeous Day

The sun beats down
There's not a cloud in the sky
No need for haste
Time drifts by
IT'S A GORGEOUS DAY

The rain pitter pats
On the window sill
Streaming rivulets
Are quiet and very still
IT'S A GORGEOUS DAY

The snow is quietly
Falling on the ground
The crystals are forming
A fascinating mound
IT'S A GORGEOUS DAY

The wind is howling
Kicking up dust
I cough and I sputter
You know I must
IT'S A GORGEOUS DAY

There is a chill in the air
It is nippy and sharp
I bundle up tight
Like a newly strung harp
IT'S A GORGEOUS DAY

I am breathing and healthy
Full of vigor and vim
I start each morning
With a happy grin
IT'S A GORGEOUS DAY

*In memory of my father, Sam Amato, who woke up
each morning and anticipated a gorgeous day!*

My Interpretation

OF ARTIST THOMAS DUNLAY'S CANVAS "SWAN BOATS IN BOSTON'S PUBLIC GARDENS"

When viewing Thomas Dunlay's canvas I do not see
Swan Boats in the Public Gardens or the grassy lea

I am drawn to a remote corner of the artists matt
Where I believe of my father in contemplation sat

There on the wooden park bench is a little old man
In a button down sweater and a cap that is tan

My thoughts go beyond the painters brush stroke
To my childhood and forgotten emotions evoked

Dad was strict and daunting yet in a loving way
He was traditionally old fashion having the last say

In hindsight he struggled with fear and insecurity
But the goodness in his heart forged his destiny

I sought independence and tried flexing my wings
In my generation it was a challenging thing

Somehow I survived those difficult days
The good times remembered the bad a haze

Dad has been at rest for many years
His legacy after drying my mournful tears

Was his love and devotion to family and friend
His honesty and compassion right to the end

My Fathers Gift

One of the greatest gifts my father gave to me
Was the courage to talk about death openly
Cancer was the reason for his drop in weight
Sad and frightened I was in a dreadful state
I could not control the onslaught of tears
Could not imagine him gone not being near
He reminded me that death was a part of life
He was grateful for his children and dear wife
He said he was not afraid of the unknown
He was ready and felt he was going home
I cried out my love saying he would be missed
He hugged me gently and gave me a sweet kiss
It is ok to be saddened and cry for a while
In time your memories should make you smile
I'm going to my maker feeling content
I gave of myself and did all that I meant
Thank you dear Daddy for your gift to me
You have helped me to face my own destiny

In loving memory

To Mom With Love

Mom…we love you so much
Your presence is like a gentle touch

The joy of you over the years
Has gladden our lives and comforted tears

We rally now at this time of your need
To do what we must in action or deed

Your mind is beautiful and still shines
But your body is on a slow decline

We rise to the occasion with love in our heart
To ease your worries and lovingly do our part

We have turned to you in joy or pain
Your words of wisdom never in vain

So Mom it is our time to protect and hold you
To lessen your burden and carry you through

We hold your hand and will not let go
This is the message we want you to know

The Real Person Inside

I know I am old!
Why?
Because I am ninety-one
That is no fun!

Deep inside
I am still a bride
I laugh, I giggle, I blush
I am in a rush
Worlds to explore
And so much more

NO!
Not a mirror!
I do not want to see
The image of me

I am the girl in my heart
Fun loving and smart
Age is just a number
I will be young until I slumber

A tribute to my mother so young at heart

"I Want To Be Me!"

(A conversation with Mom)

I want to be me!
Independent and free
The girl in my head!
…..but instead…..

My feet do not do
What I command them to
Fingers and hands …fumble
Making me….mumble

When my mind plays a trick
I must be quick
To capture an illusive thought
……...or not…..

I see 'the *me*' of yesteryear
Happy the memories are still there
Yes, I want to be the other me
But, alas that cannot be!!

Wisdom puts wishful thinking aside
Thankfully it has been a great ride
We deal with life in our own way
I chose to laugh; not cry each day

Grateful for my blessings then and now
I face my destiny with a smile and a bow!

Love you Mom…..an inspiration to the end

Saying Goodbye

"When it is time for me to leave…you must let me go!"
Mom's consoling words to me even as I thought NO!
We put aside unhappy thoughts that bring on fear and pain
Knowing the day will come when there will be some rain
From earliest childhood memories going through the years
You brought comfort and wiped away my troubled tears
Years go by seasons change and our roles become reversed
Now it is my turn to protect and love as you did at the first
The time has come to say goodbye but never in my heart
You will be there forevermore as from the start

A Message From Dad

(Delivered through Barbara)
Ethel dear it is okay
Stop the fight
I'll lead the way
See the light
Open the door
We will be together as before
Leave behind pain and sorrow
Join me in the new tomorrow
Hand in hand as it should be
Come my dear I will set you free

Barbara dear, it is okay to cry
It is time to say good-by

Take My Hand

Take my hand at heaven's door
To be united as before
Released from the longest night
Guided towards the golden light
Free of pain and infirmity
Seeing each other as we used to be
Floating through fields of flowers
Not bounded by time in hours
Frolicking in a carefree way
Joy and happiness fill each day
Time to leave our celestial home
Seeking a new lifetime in which to roam
Do not fret my dear beloved
Our soul love will be rediscovered
When it is time for our rebirth
We will find each other here on earth

*A channeled message from Sam to Ethel
thru their daughter, Barbara*

Together Forever

Following the dictates of my heart
Predetermined from the start
I will find you in each lifetime
Our destinies are so entwined
The ease in which we do the dance
This attraction is not by happenstance
When you embark on a journey anew
My spirit will not be far from you
Our light shines through eternity
The guiding stars bring you to me

Dedicated to my parents Sam and Ethel
Who have and will enjoy many lifetimes together

Remembering Mom

In hindsight
And through the hourglass of time passed
I see you in a more spiritual light
Recognizing in your lifetime
You elevated to a higher self
I recall your thoughtful words of wisdom
Your strength and selflessness
Your capacity to comfort those
In their neediest moments
Being nonjudgmental in action and deed
The shared confidences never to be violated
Countless acts of love and compassion
Remembering your serene smile
I embrace your goodness
In honoring your memory
I will endeavor to carry on your legacy

At Peace

You told me I would be okay
And see beauty in each new day

You showed how to live a fulfilling life
Taught me to smile through joy and strife

I know in my heart you are in a better place
The legacy you left puts a smile on my face

Memories of you bring comfort and peace
My love and devotion will never cease

You are with Dad through eternity
Both watching protectively over me

I am content you are together again
Someday I will join you I know not when

I am at peace and will honor you
Making you proud in all that I do

Mom's everlasting legacy

You Live On

You live on in light
A memory etched in my mind
The essence of you
That beautiful spirit
Your soul
That part that never dies
Touches your loved ones
A continuum
You
That love
That Godliness
That spark
Never ends but is passed on
And will live in generations to come
You are a comforting light
That shines in my heart

Chapter 7
Family And Friends

FATED JOURNEYS

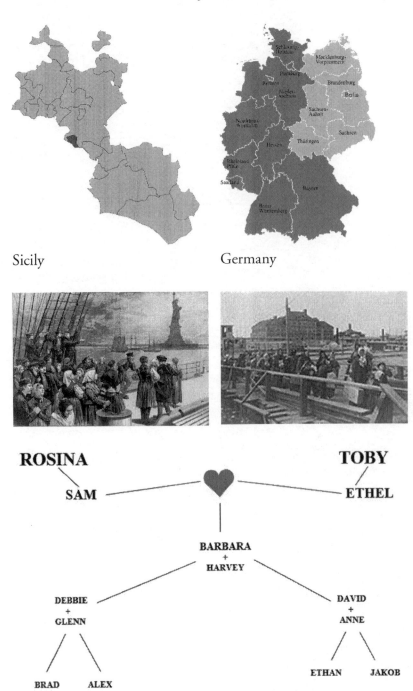

Toby And Rosina's Journey

Toby and Rosina came to America as young girls
In their prim little dresses and tight wavy curls
They traveled bravely leaving their families behind
Coming to the New World their destinies to find

Toby came from Poland with Nathan her son
Her husband sent for her after World War One
He was a stranger to her now after so many years
She left her family wiping away sorrowful tears

Rosina was a young maiden barely eighteen
Leaving the shores of Sicily it felt like a dream
She left poverty too many mouths to be fed
Sent to America an arranged husband to wed

Two young women unknown to each other
Journeyed to a future fated to bring them together
They settled in Boston's historical West End
A melting pot of nationalities strangers and friend

Toby shined in investing and housing realty
Her lodging on Lynde Street was a fine B & B
Rosina was able to write in her native tongue
Her translating skills were sought by everyone

They raised their children toiling night and day
Not knowing how to do it any other way
So different in religion yet so much the same
In valued work ethic and pride in their name

Toby's daughter Ethel and Rosina's son Sam
Met attending a swinging forties dance jam
They broke tradition with their undying love
God smiled and blessed the union from above

Later when I made my joyous welcomed debut
Bubbe and Nonna together greeted me too

*Dedicated in loving memory to my grandmothers
Toby Weiner and Rosina Amato*

My Unique Upbringing

In quiet moments I reflect on my life
I recall good times and times of strife
The sweetest joy and fondest memory
Is time shared with my wonderful family
When I close my eyes as tight as I am able
I am seated at an unconventional dining table
Dad fashioned two saw horses with planks
So much laughter as we offered thanks
Bubbe serving up her famous gifilte fish
Followed by pot roast, chicken and knish
Nonna appears serving meatballs in my reverie
While my cousins decorate the Christmas tree
Easter would find us excitedly at Nonna's door
As she gave us our biscotti baskets and more
At Passover Seder Uncle Eddie would officiate
His abbreviated service we would all appreciate
Dad would prepare his famous lobster and squid
With the uninhibited enthusiasm of an excited kid
Picnics and grand fireworks on the fourth of July
Labor Day ends summer leisure with a woeful sigh
Thankful family young and old spent holidays together
Never hampered by the threat of inclement weather
Grateful to God who smiled approvingly from above
A perfect blending of cultures sharing food and love

*While growing up it did not occur to me how
unusual was the loving acceptance.
Both sides Jewish and Italian appreciated and supported the differences.
I hope I have passed on embracing all cultures to my children.*

Nonna's Sewing Table

Nonna's table has been passed down to me
It is special for its cherished and dear memory

Running my hands over the smooth fine grain
I recall Nonna's joys and some times of pain

Seen from the eyes of a young bashful child
Her presence was formidable until she smiled

With hugs and squeezes she pinched my cheeks
Proclaiming I had grown in a matter of weeks

When tantalizing aromas in the kitchen were strewn
I knew my gurgling stomach would be filled very soon

Welcoming "coma here, I'va gotta treat for you"
Offering biscotti's, "helpa yourself taka two"

Nonna's English was broken and not very good
The love in her words was clearly understood

She crocheted booties and mastered embroidery
Remnants of her delicate work I display joyfully

It was with maturity many years later I realized
She toiled with arthritic hands and weary eyes

It has been many decades since Nonna passed away
But her sweet and loving memory is here to stay

Inspired by Nonna's sewing table that I saved from leaving the family and fond memories of my grandmother, Rosina Lapadoro Amato

To Spend A Day With You

*(Author Mitch Albom posed this question.
I was inspired to write about my grandmother)*

If a loved one could come back to spend a day with you
Who would you wish for and what would you do
I would wish for my grandmother, my beloved Bubbe
To spend those precious twenty four hours with me
I would be by her side as she sat on her favorite chair
Hold her hand and treasure the moments having her near
I would tell her stories of how I lived my life
Taking pride as a good friend, mother and wife
Tell her about her great grandchildren David and Deb
And all the amazing things that happened since I wed
All grown she would be pleased with the spouses they chose
Judaism was embraced that door did not close
Her great great grandchildren a joy beyond measure
Brad, Alex, Ethan and Jakob God's gifts and our treasure
I would use these moments comforted by her sweet embrace
To finally understand the sadness that lined her face
There was never a chance for a proper good bye
She will live in my heart until the day I die

Epilogue:

Dedicated to my beloved grandmother, Toby Weiner. She passed away the year after I married. During my adolescence I enjoyed our visits but I was too immature and she was too saddened by the Holocaust which took all members of her family for us to have any meaningful talks. Much to my regret.

A Father's Day Thank You

Sometimes it takes a special day
To stop and reflect and silently pray

To express our thanks big and small
And really appreciate the greatest gift of all

You have given me a life many would with envy deem
Showering me with riches beyond my wildest dream

I applaud your talents and generosity
But the simplest things mean the most to me

So as we celebrate your special day
It is with sincere homage and love that I say

Thank you for the best gift you ever gave
Thanks for my beloved Debbie and Dave

For without you they would not exist
They truly are my most prized gift

With gratitude I resoundingly say
You are the greatest!

HAPPY FATHERS DAY

A Father's Day Issue

As Father's Days come and Father's Day go
I have concern I thought you should know

Your attention to me has always been exemplary
With handyman skills stellar and legendary

However there is an area where you do fall short
I have exhausted all measures this is my last resort

I am at my wits end and just cannot ignore
Your dang, darn, grating irritating snore

That vibrating annoying rumbling sound
Follows me through the night round and round

I have tried gently nudging to jabs in the ribs
I have rolled and pushed you but nothing gives

I have use ear plugs, headsets and Tylenol PM
Still the sound resonates like a dozen fierce men

Whether you lie left side right side or on your chest
The irritating snoring continues with renewed zest

I am resigned and accept my destined fate
Because for me you are still the perfect mate

Truth be known we do let many annoyances pass
I am grateful you take no issue when I produce gas

Happy Birthday Harvey-2003

Your birthday is a perfect time
To say I love you with a rhyme

The day we met you took my breath away
We were attracted in that special way

I remember when you turned twenty-one
We dined at Giro's and had so much fun

You love to celebrate with pomp and flare
The challenge is to top them year after year

You are amusingly special and so unique
You love opening presents or just sneak a peak

Savoring cake and frosting presents and balloons
You anticipate the day it can't get here to soon

You do not conceal the child within
You make us all pause and warmly grin

You are bighearted and fun and love to share
With all friends and family you hold so dear

So we raise our glass and want to say
You are wished good health and
A happy birthday!

Happy Birthday Harvey-2005

Your friends marked their calendars with the date
To gather for fun and foolishness and celebrate
It would not seem like summer birthday time
If we didn't get together to toast you and dine
This year we are doing a progressive dinner
The gang thinks the plan is an award winner
Starting at the Geltman's for hors'doeuvres
At our house the main course will be served
Pam and Stephen are just down the street
For tea and coffee and a decadent treat
We will sing some songs and play a game
Anything less would be a crying shame
Kissing good bye and shouting good cheer
Let's plan to celebrate same time next year

Happy Birthday Harvey-2017

This picture sums up so much about you. From the moment we met your hero status started and continued throughout the years as I watched your curious sense of adventure bring you delight as you pursued and shared many escapades.

My life was very sheltered before you arrived on the scene. You helped me conquer so many fears. Whoever thought that a little Jewish girl from the ghetto would actually fly in a single engine aircraft and then be encouraged to take lessons or the unthinkable actually suiting up like a real biking babe and ride behind you on a motorcycle. The only thing that stopped me from learning to drive the bike was I was vertically challenged. That didn't stop you from teaching me all the fundamentals.

You helped me conquer so many fears. Over the years you challenged me to reach beyond my anxieties enabling me to experience the rush… the giddiness…the euphoria…the sense of accomplishment that so many go through life without ever experiencing.

You usually are the first to offer a helping hand and I know once something gets on the "to do" list the ink is barely dry and it's done.

You meet challenges with courage and daring…and truth be known I love the twinkle in your eyes and your engaging dimples which is usually a forerunner to something mischievous.

Happy Birthday to the love of my life. You have made the ride very interesting.

In Honor Of Our 50th Wedding Anniversary

As the orchestra plays the Anniversary Waltz refrain
Let us take a nostalgic stroll down memory lane
We met in 1959 of my high school senior year
We were young and innocent without a care
I went to Northeastern University and you to BU
Rocked to American Bandstand, Elvis and the Beatles too
You traded your Vespa for a Renault Dauphine
It was the sleekest coolest car we had ever seen
You coaxed me to fly in a Piper Cub airplane
My life since then has never been the same
You took me out of my self-imposed comfort zone
Had me soaring the blue skies or even biking alone
I hope I brought out your sensitive gentler side
Your creative energy made me burst with pride
Cantor Gordon married us at the Bell House in 1962
A honeymoon in Lake Tahoe what a breathtaking view
Our first apartment was in Downey a suburb of LA
We worked at North American Aviation together each day
The California days were leisurely with freedom to roam
But we missed our family and close friends back home
We settled back in Boston to start our family
Living in Walpole with Debbie, David and Heidi
The years have gone by and the kids are all grown
We cannot figure out where the time has flown
We are the proud grandparents of boys totaling four
Who are extraordinarily exceptional and we adore
We have resided in Wayland, Venice and Cape Cod too
Where we lived not as important as sharing with you
The essential things continue without change
For me your simple gestures are not so strange

Your eyes light up when I walk into a room
As they did when you were a bridegroom
We still hold hands in the movie show
You love my Italian cooking and tell me so
We laugh and polk fun at silly inside jokes
We still share our dreams and all our hopes
We have worked very hard as most folks do
Our love and respect carried us through
It has been a partnership with highs and lows
As we fulfilled our destiny in the life we chose
When we reflect back at what we have done
Even with all our endeavors it still was fun
I was correct knowing after our first date
That I had found my destined soul mate
Let us raise our champagne glass and toast to life
Thankful God has blessed us as husband and wife

50 years
9/3/1962-9/3/2012

Celebrating 55 Years

Our anniversary weekend is a perfect time
To express love in my trademark rhyme

I searched and searched hoping to find
The perfect card to convey my mind

I rejected the ones too comical or trite
They were not me and didn't feel right

Then it hit me I realized with a start
I am the only one who knows my heart

Realizing God has blessed us from above
My words impart thankfulness and love

We worked together in building our life
Powered by joy of being husband and wife

The secret of 55 years of wedded bliss
Is to end each night with a hug and kiss

To say I love and appreciate you
Supporting each other in all that we do

HAPPY ANNIVERSARY
1962-2017

My Dear Sister Janet

HAPPY BIRTHDAY

The earliest memory I have of you
Is a stroller ride down Blue Hill Avenue
You were tiny and cute in hand me down clothes
With dark blond ringlets and turned up nose
Even though Bubbe lamented you had "kronka" eyes
You drew lots of attention and envious sighs
Larry and I went through the gang up on you stage
The good news it was a short lived phase
I entered my teen years with you in tow
You copied my style eagerly wanting to grow
You lovingly attended me on my wedding day
I felt the love more than words could say
I moved to California for a couple of years
I missed you so much it brought me to tears
There is much I respect and admire about you
You were never afraid to try something new
At age thirty you became an honored Bat Mitzvah
A Bachelor's degree followed to fulfil your star
Your commitment to Judaism holds no bounds
It is where your source of strength is found
No one could accuse you of being a loafer
You even tried your hand at becoming Kosher
Amy and Alison are the product of you
They make you proud in whatever they do
Ella, Sam, John, Grace and Tyler what can I say
Put a contented smile on your face everyday
Your marriage to Rick is the frosting on the cake
Together in life's joys you gratefully partake
Your goodness and attributes show no end
You are a wonderful sister and my best friend

Happy 50Th Anniversary
Jan and Rick

The traditional anniversary cards celebrating
50 years didn't feel special enough and were
too trite and generic…then I saw a card
which depicts newlyweds dancing after sharing
vows and beginning their journey
together full of anticipation and wonderment….
and that seemed more appropriate to send to you…
Why?....because when I looked at that card
I also saw the couple 50 years hence and thought
of both of you and saw what love had accomplished….
Challenges were thrown in your path as well as blessings…
you have met them all so admirably. Your love and
devotion have sustained you throughout your
journey and that same bond will continue into the future.
We wish you a continuation of lives blessings,
good health and the deserved praise…"Job well done"
In the words of Mom and Dad who are always in our
thoughts especially on this wonderful occasion….
"You're a credit to society"

Brother Lost Brother Found

My brother has always been special to me
I was age ten when he joined the family
More than a brother he was like a son
Watching him grow was so much fun
The bond between us will always be there
Through stormy days or weather fair
Of late my brother and I have been lost
A tragedy of sorrow and heart felt cost
We take different and separate roads
As our journey through life continues to unfold
I look forward to our paths touching again
I know it will happen I know not when
What consoles me most day after day
Is knowing he is in my heart to stay

Epilogue:

My heart is filled with joy. My brother and I found each other again and our lives are enriched. The best part our mother's last years were peacefully content knowing her children had rekindled their relationship.

Debbie

The occasion of your birthday is a perfect time
To write my reminiscences in a special rhyme

Your father and I were proud as could be
When the doctor said we soon would be three

Anticipating your arrival brought us much joy
It did not matter if you were a girl or boy

I recall so fondly your pending birth
Excitement allowed me to overlook my girth

You finally arrived and it was like a dream
You were the cutest baby I had ever seen

We brought you home in our Volkswagen Beatle
Dad drove so slow people thought he was feeble

I was so nervous I nearly fell down on my knees
When during the night you hiccupped and sneezed

By some miracle we survived the first trying night
We learned and grew together as I held you tight

I was thoroughly in love with my sweet little girl
From the tip of your toes to that stubborn curl

When the doctors diagnosed a serious problem hip
You taught us courage by the smile on your lip

You loved to help me with my cleaning chores
Like a little mother you tried to dust the floors

It didn't surprise us even though you were tiny
That your first few worlds were 'clean and shiny'

You always showed individuality and good taste
Protecting the environment or frowning at waste

The years flew by as we watched you grow
A kaleidoscope of images that blend and glow

From the first day of school to sweet sixteen
Then off to college on wings and a dream

Your accomplishments brought me great pride
Especially your marriage and Glenn by your side

Together you gave me Alex and Brad
The most special gift a mother could have

In reflection and gratitude I can humbly say
God truly blessed me on your birth day

Happy 25th Wedding Anniversary Debbie And Glenn

As you embark upon and celebrate your 25 years of marriage, we can still see our little girl walking down the aisle with joy and anticipation into the awaiting arms of a man who stood tall beaming with pride as his bride seemed to float toward him and their future. It was a beautiful and heartwarming vision then and now twenty-five years later we see it as a dreams come true journey with well-earned pride in all you two have accomplished.

Marriage is not an easy ride. Along with the smooth ribbons of highway there are bumps and turns and unexpected detours along the way. What we have noticed is how you both have worked together in a wonderful partnership figuring out what is best for you and your family. Throughout the years we have heard laughter, seen hugging and expressions of love and caring.

You have set an excellent example for Brad and Alex which accounts so much for their kind and loving natures. They are bright, hardworking adults now with great futures ahead of them. Their legacy and dreams will be attained due to your commitment and fulfillment of vows you made twenty five years ago.

We honor you both as you celebrate your 25th anniversary. May your love continue to be aglow, may you both be healthy, and may happiness and God's blessings be in your future.

A Note To Brad And Alex

For all those occasions you shined through the year
Claiming honors and prizes to resounding cheer
Here is a little extra spending money
Don't laugh we are not being funny
Buy something really differently bazaar
Or parlay it into a shiny sports car
Okay we're joking to make the rhyme
You realize an auto is on your dime
But there is one thing we shout out loud
The both of you have made us real proud

Epilogue:

It is now 10 years later. Brad is in his third year of medical school and Alex has a BS in Liberal Arts, a Master's in Business and CPA certification. They are well on their way to purchasing their shiny new sport cars.

David

When I reflect remembering you as a child
I recall a young boy who easily smiled
A baby content to cuddle and softly coo
As if hiding secrets without giving a clue

Never requiring the attention of center stage
A quality that remained the same even with age
You easily gave acquaintances their just due
The limelight was something foreign to you

Non-confrontational in manner and a quick wit
Making others laugh and hoot with a noisy arm pit
You participated in school sports but didn't excel
Being part of a group or team worked very well

You were smart not nerdy and sought out for fun
Easy going and amiable you became number one
The dynamic trait that surfaced year after year
An ability to encourage others to rise for the cheer

Brilliant and wise your IQ way off the chart
Never diminished your caring and giving heart
Teachers recognized they had a gifted student in you
Knowing you would accomplish what you set out to do

In junior year which was pivotal if college bound
You taught yourself Physics when no teacher was found
You procrastinated submitting applications for college
Your one overture, offered, impressed with your knowledge

Attending prestigious MIT gave you the foundation
To pursue medicine with vigor and determination

Drinking with the guys downing a beer or two
You became the go-to person to replenish the brew

Those years prepared you to enter medical school
You balanced smarts with lots of fun nobody's fool
The years that followed you earned many a degree
An MD Oncologist and an Immunology PHD

We are proud and pleased it is needless to say
But the best gift you gave us nearly blew us away
It is our daughter in law Anne your lovely bride
She completes your life as your journey side by side

If that's not enough there's icing on the cake
Our wonderful grandchildren Ethan and Jake
Today you are leading finding the cancer cure
Immune oncology the pathway for that special door

I knew your gift would lead to something great
Making the world better will be your amazing fate

Another Special Thank You To My Son

My pride in you grows day after day
Why are you so special?
Well I will put it this way!

As the years tick by one after another
You indulge a little quirk of your mother

You close your eyes and agree that it is fine
And allow me to be only thirty-nine

Instant Love

Welcome little one yes this is the place
You found us as you journeyed through space

Your arrival prompted joy and great fanfare
We knew it was fate that brought you here

Showers of stardust sprinkled from above
We saw each other and it was instant love

Welcome to the family
Ethan

Gramps And Me

I am a lucky fella
I will tell you why
Gramps whispered in my ear
We can fly to the sky

We can play choo choo
And crawl on the floor
We can play ball and tent
When I say more more

Gramps is so tall
But I am not afraid
He puts me on his shoulders
And we watch the parade

I see the pretty flowers
Gramps says pick only one
I look at him sweetly
I know he will succumb

Gramps loves me
I know it is true
When I fall down
He kisses my boo boo

Gramps hugs and tickles me
And calls me little man
He finds my blankey
When I frantically can't

When I am older
He will teach me his tools
But for now I must watch
Sucking my fingers with drool

It is time for night night
I do not want to go
Gramps pats my head
And says that's how I will grow

I go to sleep
With happy thoughts
Cause I know tomorrow
We will play a lot

I love you, Gramps

Ode To Ethan

Ethan will be visiting we can hardly wait
To prepare for the visit went to bed at eight

We have taken our vitamins and rested well
Determined not to go down with the bell

Bye mommy and daddy ready for fun and games
With Gram it books with Gramps it is planes

For the first hour we kept up with the tike
Oh no now he wants to go on his bike

Up and down the street having fun no doubt
Please slow down you are wearing us out

You pause for apple juice and a little snack
Energized you gleefully hurry back

Nappy time cannot come too soon
Yes, we are mindful it is only noon

You are up again and gearing for fun
Oh dear can it only be quarter past one

We take shifts now it is the only way
To make it through this very long day

The clock says seven a wonderful sight
Let us get him in pj's it is almost night

Bathy proved to be time for alarm
He nearly squiggled out of my arm

Powder and pamper and smelling so sweet
Hug and squeeze him and tickle his feet

Grab his worn blankey and favorite toy
Routine is the same whether girl or boy

He struggles and fights sleep all the way
Slumber wins out rest up for another day

Smiling tired and weary good night little dove
We'd do it again gladly that's the power of love

Ethan's Poem

*(Inspired when Ethan age 9 said
he could turn junk into a dream)*

Don't throw that broken bike away
I'll save its parts for another day
That boogie board splintered in two
Can I borrow it from you?
A piece of old fencing bent a bit
Snuggly under my bed will fit
My imagination holds no bound
Thinking of all the stuff I have found
Shall I fashion a cool rocket ship
For an inter-galactic space trip
Or maybe build a sleek sports car
With headlights from a pickle jar
Things are not what they seem
"I can turn junk into a dream"

Epilogue:

*Ethan is 16 now and embarking on
an interesting journey in aviation.*

Welcome Jakob

Your birth at five twenty-eight on January third
Was the best news we could have heard

You arrived early as quick as could be
To take your special place in the family

Born in Manhattan in crowded New York
This did not hinder the dispatching stork

You have a terrific mother and really cool dad
Your older brother Ethan is a fun little lad

Your Grandparents are in love with you
They will take pride in whatever you do

You have aunts and uncles and cousins galore
Many adventures when you are ready to explore

For now little one rest growing big and strong
Knowing you are surrounded with love all day long

Epilogue:

Jakob is 14 now. His passion and dedication to gymnastics has evolved since age 7. Today he is ardently training to qualify for the 2020 Maccabi Games in Israel.

Ethan And Jakob On Their Bar Mitzvahs

HONORING ETHAN

Your grandfather and father pass the Torah to you
Symbolizing your passage as a responsible Jew
We honor your strengths and accomplishment
Watching you embark on this life cycle event
As a Bar Mitzvah you accept the Torah teaching
Its significance in your life will be far reaching
We celebrate you with great joy pride and love
May God protect and bless you from above

April 12, 2014

HONORING JAKOB

As Jakob becomes 'Son of Commandment' on this special day
He will chant his Haftorah and lead the congregation to pray
His responsibility to carry on Jewish tradition has begun
With a 3000 year old ritual of passing Torah father to son
This milestone will have meaning throughout his life
He will draw from his teachings in happiness and strife
His family and friends gather with support and love
Bestowing well earned praise and joyful Mazel Tov!

January 3, 2016

The Uniqueness Of The Day You Were Born

On the day of your birth
You gifted the world with your presence
On your birthday
We recognize the uniqueness of the day
A day to celebrate you!
Calls and cards from family and friends
Are a wonderful expression of their love
And your special place in their hearts
It has become clear to me that age represents
The time we have graced this earth
And it is *our* gift to others
So…on the day you were born
Your special day
We celebrate you and
Appreciate and recognize
Your special gifts
and
What a blessing you are!

Always remember you are a
Cherished gift from God
and
You reflect His goodness

To One and All
HAPPY BIRTH DAY

Honoring Aunt Molly
ON HER 80TH BIRTHDAY

Auntie Molly you are great and unlike any other
To me you were always like a second mother

On that cold winter night when I came on the seen
You were a bobby soxer and cool Frank Sinatra teen

Your chic style and uniqueness we lovingly adore
You worked at sales at Gilchrist Department store

Most of my memories involve you and Uncle Eddie
From my wedding rescue to ketchup on spaghetti

Leaving work when motherhood called you to duty
A natural mother you lovingly raised Carl and Judy

A new career brought you legend at Boston University
Your face "mask" adorned the wall for posterity

Grandchildren Brad and Alex are the frosting on your cake
Your love devotion and memories through life they will take

Throughout my life you have always been there
My go to person offering support and loving care

Happy birthday to someone special, doting and jolly
There is no one like you my wonderful Auntie Molly

Epilogue:

*Auntie Molly passed away in November, 2011
caring and loving, feisty and worldly, right to the end.*

The In-Laws

In-laws are individuals who come to you
Through your children after they say I do

An in-law relationship might not stick
If they're folks you might not naturally pick

The word even conjures a knowing smile
Upon hearing it some want to run a mile

There are stories and jokes and lots of hype
Luckily our in-laws are not your stereotype

We discovered interests and common ground
Love to be with them and just hang around

We literally spend hours and not get bored
Discussing grandchildren mutually adored

We are so fortunate and thankfully say
A bond was formed on our kids wedding day

So grateful to our children we really owe 'em
For presenting us with the best MUKATONEM*

**The Yiddish word that describes the
unique relationship between the parents of
the bride, Barbara and Harvey and
the groom, Norma and Ron*

Grace Ann

Welcome Grace Ann
Home at last
To the loving arms of
Your family

Grace
Homage to yesterday
Harmony the morrow
Connection, continuity
Rebirth

Mother and child
Basking in glorious delight
Pampered fluff of femininity
Oh, joy

Kindred spirit embrace protect
Surrounded in love's radiant light
Sprinkled with stardust
Celestial gifts bestowed

Determination, grace
Compassion, wisdom
Freedom to be
Yourself

Soar on wings
Strong and sure
Mindful when in flight
Your destiny awaits

Grace
Special, unique
With your own gifts
To give the world

Welcome to the family
Grace Ann

John Hanks A Talented Man

John started his career on the flying trapeze
Soaring through the air with the greatest of ease

Soon those strong hands that could not be still
Toiled creatively to develop his carpentry skill

God gave him a special gift magnificently grand
A technical brain along with a talented hand

He has three dimensional insight and ability
To envision and construct a project mentally

He takes a piece of wood with a delicate grain
And fashions it into art easily without a strain

His artistry is sought by many far and wide
By reputation he's known across the country side

When family is in trouble and need his expertise
He is there to solve the problem fast like a breeze

When others give up a task in despair
John tool box in hand says I'll be there

He is a teacher and helper right to the end
It is an honor to call you our good friend

New Definition Of Family

Today defining family is open for interpretation
This notion in the past denied without explanation

A typical family was headed by a dad and mother
Together raising siblings sister and brother

The discussion now ensues how we analyze and define
The composition of a family in this day and time

When the well-being of the family unit is the goal
There should be no limits in identifying the role

Grandparents have risen to take responsibility
When parents are unable to offer care and stability

Notably same gender parents are doing just fine
In raising children who are loving and kind

Caring friends who offer home and security
Help children reach their potential and maturity

Children grow to become what they have lived
A product of the love and teaching you give

When people come together in a caring way
No matter how defined FAMILY is here to stay

The Gift Of Friendship

The gift of friendship comes from the heart
No wrapping paper or ribbons to pull apart
It is not a bauble to wear on finger or neck
Nor ticket to cruise or mountain to trek
It is not seen or displayed on a pedestal
Played with or pampered at whim or will
A friend is more precious than shiny gold
It is a blessing and a pleasure to behold
A relationship natural and met with ease
No need for pretense excuses or apologies
There for you with a compassionate ear
A shoulder for a burden and painful tear
Rejoicing when good fortune makes a call
Overlooking failings imperfections and all
It is priceless and cherished and is earned
Happily given and then lovingly returned

Friendships
(Long Time or New)

Old friendships are precious and held dear
Built on the life's experiences that we share

Bolstering and caring for each other as we age
Celebrating sadness and joys at every stage

New friends are made as our journey unfolds
Appreciated but not to replace our treasured old

Each enrich and enhance our odyssey through life
Exchanging insights during happiness and strife

A bond is established with mutual camaraderie
Respecting and enjoying each other's company

A friendship is not measured in time spent together
But by being there when needed by one or the other

It should not be a challenge or popularity contest
But a reciprocal feeling of emotion and interest

Whether couched in longevity or relatively new
The gift of a true friend is a blessing to you

Pamela

Intimate with Natures wonder
In the touch of earth
In nurturing
In sweat and resolve
In pleasure of beauty

Seeker of color and texture
In rainbows wondrous pallet
Shining through hands
Strong and sensitive
Honesty… determination… boldness

Sheltering arms
Enfold in comforting embrace
Protective hands reach out
Gently stroking
Unconditional love

Reserved humor
In twinkled eyed merriment
In dignity and quiet vulnerability
Unique convergence into
Oneness

Tapestry of life
A weaving intricate and simple
Sturdy resilient lasting
Threads of love entwined
Peace

"Pamela" the essence of the woman whom
I admire and whose friendship I treasure

Happy Birthday Pearl

I am pleased to celebrate this special day with you
And reflect on the years and how they flew
No matter your age you will always be
That young vibrant girl in my memory
I treasure our friendship and times we share
And look forward to celebrating year after year

Pearl's Courage

Like a bolt from out of the blue
A life changing event happened to you
A lesser person might have fallen apart
You have shown grit and lots of heart
You did not break down or shy away
You plunged head on to slay the prey
For weeks it was difficult and not fun
You met the challenge and got the job done
I admire your courage under adversity
You are the most amazing woman to me

Our friendship goes back to high school days.
It is a treasured gift

Sidney And Samantha

IN HONOR OF YOUR B'NAI MITZVAH

There are twin sisters cute as can be
Loaded with spunk and personality
Thirteen years ago their story began to unfold
Bringing smiles and joy and dreams untold
Jewish coming of age has a special mission
To maintain an unbroken chain of tradition
A *B'nai Mitzvah* is a blessing times two
With someone who is always there for you
It may not necessarily be twice as much fun
But it helps knowing you are not the only one
Your love ones will *kvell* and burst with pride
As you stand at the *bimah* side by side
So congratulations and *mazel tov*
This poem is sent with all my love

*Dedicated to our dear friends Bob and Joan
whose granddaughters inspired this poem*

Call Me Old-Fashion

I know we are in the electronic age
When sending E-cards is the rage
Call me old-fashion but it seems more real
To send a card that you can read and feel
You search and reject until the perfect one
That reflects your personality and zest for fun
It expresses appreciation for all you do
And states my special love for you
It is signed with a message from the heart
That conveys my feelings from the start

Chapter 8
Retirement

New Beginnings

AN INSPIRING WAY TO ENVISION RETIREMENT

A new beginning is just outside your door
New found freedoms to uncover and explore

Lost in search of a new and exciting identity
Look within for more insight and clarity

You are not defined by status or career
The essence of you is special and held dear

First settle in and then lazily drift along
Try your hand at creating a melodic song

Change is important and good you see
Use it to harness and tap into new energy

Sit back and enjoy the slower easier pace
Relax be creative you are not in a race

Travel a new road and exciting avenue
Savor life and options as you start anew

Eternal Youth

Experience youth no matter your age
By acting young at heart at any stage

Laugh and sing and shout with joy
Applies equally whether girl or boy

Staying young starts in your head
Act not like a senior think kid instead

Go ahead ride the carnival Ferris wheel
Scream with delight if it is how you feel

There is no elixir or medicine to take
Just appreciate life's joys and partake

Retirement

Retirement should be your time for play
You paid your dues and earned your pay

Seek daybreak cycling over hill and dale
Or a sunset spin using rudder and sail

Try your hand with an easel paint and brush
Take your time and savor there is no rush

Join a lively group chorus and sing a song
Play weekly games of canasta or mahjongg

Volunteer to share your hobbies or skill
Romping with grandchildren what a thrill

Winter winds bring you to a warmer clime
So caravan down south for the winter time

At the end of the day be grateful and content
A peaceful weariness for a day well spent

Fond memories and images forever keep
When you lay your head down to sleep

Happy Retirement Harvey

In honor of my husband on his retirement
I wrote a poem to commemorate the event

It seems like yesterday with diploma in hand
You set out to make a difference in our land

You found your niche and did incredibly well
Guiding missiles to where the enemies dwell

They were deployed with the utmost accuracy
You did it with confidence, pride and veracity

You worked well with branches of the military
A diplomatic juggling act and sometimes scary

I proudly witnessed the government bestow upon you
A lifetime achievement acknowledging all you do

Only a handful of people have been honored this way
You accepted humbly saying "I'm just earning my pay"

Your entrepreneurial drive would not abate
You parlayed a laundromat into prime real estate

You have entered a new stage so relax and enjoy
With golf clubs and cameras you are a lucky boy

You have time for travel and being with the kids
Working on endless chores that sometimes slid

You will complete projects numbering ten or eleven'
Woefully, my new role has me on twenty-four seven

Farewell Woburn Medical Associates

Work life goes on at such a hectic pace
We do what we must it is part of the race

The time has come to pursue new dreams
To step off the track and follow a new beam

Saying goodbye is trying and very difficult task
The significance is life changing and hard to grasp

If memories are treasures I'm rich beyond belief
If I touched you a little I'm filled with relief

Alas I bid farewell with a tear and a smile
Images and friendships will last a long while

I leave with pride my head held high
Fulfilling my dream to reach for the sky

Think of me fondly I am that imaginary dot
Remember my words of wisdom fill one more
Slot!

I was employed by Woburn Medical Associates as their first Practice Administrator from 1986 to 2003. The visionary was Dr. Marsha Wade who hired me to grow her practice from four Internal Medicine Subspecialty doctors. When I retired from WMA we operated out of two locations consisting of 11 Primary Care physicians with subspecialties in Cardiology, Nephrology, Oncology, Pulmonology and Gastroenterology, 6 Nurse Practitioners, Registered Nurses, Medical Assistants and ancillary staff. We had a full service clinical laboratory including bone density testing, ultrasound technology and in-office endoscopy. I was instrumental in bringing manage care into our community hospital working in partnership creating the first PHO (Physician Hospital Organization) at Winchester Hospital our local community hospital.

Thank You Woburn Medical

Thank you for my party it was really great
So much work went into helping me celebrate

Tasteful decorations with colorful balloons
Flowers and streamers covered the room

Shrimp and veggies lots of healthy food
Put me in a special festive party mood

Nothing forgotten we even had wine
I got a little tipsy but that was fine

Many friends and coworkers wishing me well
It brought tears and smiles you could tell

The cake so decadent I wanted to scream
Chocolate and vanilla and so much cream

Oh! What presents surprise after surprise
Starting with crystal that squinted my eyes

Flowers and plants, books, pens, and vases
Gift cards for shopping or dining in fine places

I could go on and on but the most difficult part
Was when I knew I had to finally leave and depart

It brought a lump to my throat and tear to my eye
I was leaving my friends and saying good-bye

The most precious and treasured gift I soon realized
As I scanned the room seeing smiles and shiny eyes

It is the people and friendships I have made
That are locked in my heart and will not fade

Thank you Woburn Medical and all my friends
Thanks for the memories they will last till the end

Our Journey

Our journey through life
Is an interesting road

As we follow the pathways
And our destiny unfolds

How we handle the roadblocks
Curves and events

Is a measure of our grace
Character and strengths

You my friend
Can look back with pride

Knowing you have touched
And enriched so many lives

May the road ahead
Be smooth and kind

May you be blessed as you
Travel to the end of time

Dedicated to Sandy Luther
In honor of her retirement

Reflections Of Kathy

We create our legacy on a meandering road
Through crossways and challenges it will unfold

Your tapestry of life is a beautiful weave
Encompassing your spirit and what you achieved

Driven by goodness and a caring heart
Your character and grace play an important part

You can look back with great joy and pride
Your courage and determination run side by side

You speak your mind in such a gentle way
With amazing insight in the words you say

The well-being of others motivates you
With purpose you accomplish what you must do

The fierceness of a lion protecting family
You are a pillar of strength and generosity

In an Irish brogue so many stories you told
Their mirth and wisdom a delight to behold

A voice of an angel you sing a sweet song
Sometimes heard throughout the night long

We toast an amazing friend, mother and wife
Grateful you have played a part in our life
Happy Retirement

Kathy Wood, coworker and friend whose upbeat philosophy of life, wisdom and caring are exemplary and whose devotion to family and friends is limitless.

Happy Retirement Cynthia

Today we honor and celebrate Cynthia on her retirement
While friends at Mutual of Omaha are filled with sentiment

She joined the team when they were Aetna twenty years ago
With the same enthusiasm and dedication we admire and know

Her ability to decipher ever changing Medicare rules
Can make uninformed providers appear like fools

Some less scrupulous providers would shiver and shake
When she discovered a cover-up or coding mistake

Her leadership skills are straight forward and true
Demonstrating values for success in all that we do

She lights up a room with her warmth and genuine smile
Encouragement and motivation are her management style

If our quarterly and target goals we did meet
The reward was a theme lunch or decadent treat

She could break a board with the flat of her hand
Or quilt an intricate blanket to be displayed on a stand

She is an intelligent woman of so many facets it is true
Like a treasured polished gem that shines like new

She attempted starting retirement once or twice
Thinking staying at home would be easy and nice

But when a company related crisis did arise
That she came back to the team was no surprise

We wish you well in this new phase of your life
Enjoy being a grandmother, mother and wife

Take leisure time to play and have some fun
You have earned the praise JOB WELL DONE!

Epilogue

Even thought I never met Cynthia, her story given to me by my daughter, Debbie, along with her request to write a poem commemorating Cynthia's retirement from Mutual of Omaha reminded me how gratifying it is be appreciated and know you have left your mark at the culmination of your working career.

Gray Hair

*A STALWORTH SIGN OF AGING AND WISDOM
OR FOR SOME
A BATTLE OF FUTILITY*

Like a trained soldier claiming newly conquered territory,
you are ready to spring at the slightest provocation.
Nerves of steel, you obtain a foothold and then
steadfastly plunge onward.
Heralded by some as a symbol of hard-earned wisdom,
you glory in the praise.
Your superiority firmly established you meet
resistance with force.
Obsessed with total vanquishment you march triumphantly
forward gaining ground with each plundering step.
Blatantly waving your banner victory is in sight!
"Stop!" I shout. *"Stop this war of attrition!"*
"Death to the traitorous enemy!"
Duty bound not to surrender,
I am spurned into retaliation.
Unscrupulous in my choice of weapons,
I deploy deadly chemical warfare.
Guiltlessly, I watch the enemy succumb to defeat,
overpowered by my potent attack.
Farwell old thwarted enemy
Farewell, yet alas not goodbye
For inevitably the fruits of victory are short lived
and we shall confront each other again
on this common battle ground.

"Till we meet again….so long!

……Gray Hair!!

Chapter 9
Travel Memories

Our Heritage

Valley hues take our breath away
As the morning sun heralds the new day
A placid stream receives a graceful bird
Neither sound nor echoes can be heard
Buffalo and bears safely lumber the trail
Birds gliding serenely over hill and dale
Trees yawn and stretch to reach the sun
Enjoying freedoms shared by every one
Mountains soaring mightily to the sky
Plump cumulus clouds gently drifting by
God has bestowed a hallowed sacred trust
In this glorious heritage presented to us
Feel the wondrous presence of His loving hand
See the miles of splendor in our blessed land
Pondering our place in the grand scheme
What does our universal existence truly mean
It is uncomplicated yet amazing profound
We must leave this sacred land as it was found

Inspired visiting Glacier National Park

Our Children's Legacy

Our children's children may never know

The smell of clean air or pure white snow
A sky that is clear without any haze
A swim in a pond and carefree days
Wildlife not mired in an oil slick
No contaminants that make them sick
The wonders of gazing at a star filled night
A tomorrow free of hunger and blight
A world with no suffering and pain
The feeling of peace after a new fallen rain

Do not rob them of life's simple pleasures
Saving the environment protects our treasures
Our duty is to preserve their legacy
To leave the world as God meant it to be

Images

As a woman city born and bred

I have fanciful images in my head

Of a place with pastures and trees

Galloping horses and a gentle breeze

Of living in an open unspoiled space

Where simplicity of nature has a place

Never did I think I would see

My whimsical fantasy become reality

Your ranch captures old and new

Acres of freedom under a sky of blue

When I wish to escape in my mind

Your horse farm in Ipswich I will find

Thank you Julie, Tony and Jo for sharing your beautiful ranch where I was left breathless enjoying your magnificent horses and viewing the simplicity of nature.

A Tourists View Of New York City

New York City is an interesting and bustling place
Where residents may lose the smile on their face
Caught up in the grind and daily routine
They forget the uniqueness of their scene
For those seeking enjoyment and diversity
Nothing compares to the vitality of New York City
Activities and adventure for every taste
Extravagant spending or impractical waste
Travel Tribeca and SoHo, East Side or West
You can always find what you like best
Brooklyn, Harlem, Queens and the Bronx
Identified easily by the cars blaring honks
Theatre for plays, museums, concerts and more
Endless attractions to culturally explore
Architectural bridges gracefully span
The island is accessible to all on land
Take a leisurely stroll down Fifth Avenue
Then pass the Plaza for a Central Park view
Ice skate at Rockefeller and enjoy the bright tree
Be a spectator viewing the Morning Show at NBC
Patronize the exclusive boutiques in upscale Manhattan
Bring wallets that dollars and credit cards have fattened
Sightsee uptown and downtown without skipping a beat
For knock-off bargains the best buy is Canal Street
Take a break for a quick bialy, bagel or nosh
When all fueled get caught up with the rush
Remember do not tire and wear yourself out
The nightlife here is the best without doubt
Get decked in black tie gown or funky attire
Celebrate until the remnants of night expire
Time to go home whether air, road or track

I shall return there will be no holding back
I am taken with the city in manner and *tork*
I have become the biggest fan when I say

I LOVE NEW YORK!!

Tanglewood In The Summer

August, 2016

In the Berkshire Hills of western Massachusetts…submerged in majestic pines and oaks…surrounded by a mountainous terrain…you will find Tanglewood. Whether sitting in the esteemed shed or folding chairs under the canvas tent, or for the adventurous, picnic style on the lawn… one can close their eyes and let other senses absorb the philharmonic sounds of the Boston Symphony Orchestra.

Transported to a timeless space, the music and the inherent message, gives us pause to reflect on our own existence. The symphonic sounds of the masters…music created from the depths of their souls speaks to us. To the insightful, through the melodic notes of great works, the blending of individual instruments into a transitional cacophony, and the interpreting direction of talented maestros, we are channeled to sounds that touch our core and usher in promise, raising us from despair to greater peaks and perhaps bringing us to a place of serenity.

Tonight homage is paid to Mahler…Gustav Mahler. His composition "What wild flowers tell me"….a country dance, a klezmer child-like transition, influences and interprets life's journey and transports the melodic dancing notes from ear to heart. A symphonic statement that weaves the sound of nature with fairy-like fanfare…reminiscent of a jaunt through colorful fragrant fields… while injecting symbols give pause for reflection and anticipation of long sunny days of summer…. a symphonic depiction of life in the orchestral movements from turbulence to triumph. We feel the parallels between life and nature whether from peaceful interludes or tumultuous overtures.

Whether you follow traditional norms or improvise as you move along your journey, you make your music from beginning to end. I have been accused of being an eternal optimist…guilty! I see fullness not empty vessels….my naivety does not blind me to life's more bleaker moments but to not embrace the positive is to give in to darkness, despair and hopelessness…I do not give in and believe in the symphonic nature of our lives…and our ability to share and show a more uplifting side is healing and encouraging and may be the instrument to lessen suffering. To our composers you are testament to that interaction and its force in life's journey.

Through our own intros, crescendos, intermezzos and encores....we hold our own baton...forces may try to take it away...hold fast... hold steady... believe in goodness... and light and music will prevail...find serenity and self-reflection and peace.

Beethoven's Ninth Symphony
AN ODE TO JOY AND CELEBRATION OF LIFE

The ninth and most significant symphony
Beethoven's joyous sounds reverberate

The metronomic cadence
Sweet sounds of symbols
Accompanying strings
Winds powerfully resonate
The maestro demands
We reach deep

Strangers unify in melodic wonder
Lips turn magically into smiles
Smiles connect
We are one

Joyously our senses fill
Music touches our core
Heart pounding crescendo
Struggles-Triumphs
Synthesized
Sweet calming intermezzo
Rejuvenating stillness
Radiating warmth

Joy of life
Peace

Exciting Tanglewood where Boston Symphony orchestra delights summer residence and visitors as their amazing sounds permeate the wooded wonderland of the Berkshires in Massachusetts

Eternal Pompeii

Journey back in Roman history
When Vesuvius claimed its progeny
A sudden fiery volcanic storm
Eerie silence no new dawn
Forgotten souls buried deep
Lonely quiet timeless sleep
Shadowy forms in the mist
Spirit world still exists
Life was not stolen away
Ethereal living day by day
Parallel lifetimes do take place
Nothing lost in time and space
We do not die and fade away
Eternal lives live on each day

*Inspired by emotions transmitted to me as
I walked the buried ancient Roman city of Pompeii.
I felt the spirit life.*

A Halo Over Mt Vesuvius

Traveling through Italy's glorious countryside
Noticing spiritual messages throughout the ride

I see a cloud hovering over Mt Vesuvius
Appearing as a golden halo sheltering us

The image projected is a protective arm
Safeguarding us from danger and harm

If you let your eyes wonder here and there
You will notice God's vigilance everywhere

His message and signs are easy to recognize
When we observe through believing eyes

Entrust your faithfulness to a higher being
Discover His touch in all you are seeing

Recognizing spiritual signs everywhere

On The Road To The Sun

Eager travelers
Move in timeless wonder
Lost in silent awe
When did the world become a carpet of color
Sun gilded peaks of silver and blue
Green ribbons of cottonwood and willow
A meadowlark sings a beckoning tune
Wild ducks and heron stealthily dive
A world fraught with predators
Life's intricate balance
Survival
Ascend
With a trespassers lightness of step
We intrude on sacred ground
A panorama of perfection
Profound stillness
Seen through the mind's eye
Not palate or camera's lens
Capture sounds
Feel the air breathe its purity
Discovery of self
Alone but not loneliness
Reverberating echoes
Infinity
Ascend
Walk the footprints of legendary lore
Wild rises of rock
Rivers steadfast thunderous roar
Powerfully carved canyons
Enthralling heights
Wonder
Giddy with adventure

Ascend
Weave through time
Explosive upheavals
Glacial storms
Infernal flares
Layers
Survival
Ascend
Rise to the apex
Burst through the splendor
Close to divinity and the majesty of God
Road's end
Home

*Inspired by our glorious excursion on the Sun Road
in Glacier National Park*

Touch The Sky

Reach out and touch the sky
Take a breath and start to fly

The higher we rise the more it is clear
We have found heaven on earth here

Feel the presence of his loving hand
In the majesty of this glorious land

Commune with God and feel as one
In this paradise under the sun

At the summit of the Road to the Sun, Montana

Where's The Bear

Over there!
Is that a bear?
Do not stare
Or get to near!
Offer no fare
Not even a pear!
If you dare
Confront your fear
With a brave cheer!
Wait, do you hear
A subtle snare?
Does he bare
A ravenous glare?
Beware!
Take care!
Retreat to the rear!

Young Side Of Old

Parasail
Hunt for quail
Bungee jump
A camel's hump
Golden years
No more fears
Exciting and so good
Second chance at childhood
Be adventurous and bold
The young side of old

Chapter 10
Poetic Therapy

A Rhyme and Reason for Behavior

Forgiveness

Forgiveness is your choice to release rage
It is positive healing effective at any age

If you wish lasting peace in your heart
Truly forgiving is a good way to start

Energy put into resentment and hate
Poisons your soul the longer you wait

Anger is a destructive corrosive disease
That robs your joy and a feeling of ease

Forgiveness does not absolve the sin
The offender works that out from within

You are saying I accept your apology
Releasing the energy holding your agony

It is the ultimate act of love mercy and grace
That will surely put a smile on your face

Choices

Our journey navigates through happiness and strife
This odyssey will continue until the end of life
Part of our adventure is driven by destinies fate
What remains are *our* choices to complete our slate
At a crossroad we ponder which direction to take
We do have choices in those decisions we make
You may decide possessions are not the sole reason
That you welcome each new and changing season
Being generous kindhearted and giving of yourself
May be more important than acquiring wealth
The choices are yours from the moment of birth
To make your mark before you leave this earth

So Speaks......A Honeydew??

Ouch! Don't thump so hard!
Hey out there!
♪ I'm r-i-p-e ♪
Boy, you must have had a bad night.
I don't plan on letting you sour my mood
No siree, I'm bursting with life and
I want to share my joy
Sit back, take a load off
You relaxed?
Okay, open wide!
Good, heh?
That's better
Glad to see you smile
Now go out there and spread a little sunshine!

Color Me What?
Preconceived notions about personality can be misleading!

To say one is a blue personality or one's nature is indicative
of a red type is unfair placing limitations on that person.

To label a person so would be as simplistic as calling
the splash of breathtaking colors in a New England
fall landscape simply "a change of season".

I reject such labels and the restrictions they impose.

Would not a gray or black personality always convey a portent
of gloom or an effervescent red a perpetual bubble of fantasy?

Auras of red or green or hues of yellow or blue
are only a captured moment of emotion.

The ability to change comes from within and herein
lies man's eternal hope. The freedom to change
and the ability to grow is our ray of hope.

I see mankind as a kaleidoscope of colors; a spectrum
of hope, fear, pain, laughter and love.

Hearing the wail of a baby's first breath, I am
reminded that he holds a rainbow in his wake.

A Parable Between Plants And People

The once vibrant bloom wilts from neglect
The dying is a prolonged painful death

Once nurtured in a tender caring way
Robbed of sustenance it withers day after day

A garden needs attention and a loving hand
Or roots slowly shrivel the stalk will not stand

People like plants share an elemental need
They thrive on loving attention and deed

We grow in the warmth of earnest praise
Indifference shortens and darkens our days

Bonds of love nourish and enrich our soul
Friendships cultivated endure as we grow old

Love is the essence of a fulfilling happy life
Sharing joy and support when there is strife

The sun shines down on those who care
Your life garden flourishes year after year

The Child Within

The child within is eager to be carefree
To experience views and spirit naturally
Remember when there was an ease in life
Before many burdens filled us with strife
Freedom as the wind blew in your hair
Biking down the steep hill without fear
Your dog and you were so very cool
As he slathered your face with sticky drool
When you were dissatisfied with your game
You shouted "do over" without any shame
How did we get so caught up in the race
We forgot simple pleasures to brighten our face
Being young at heart is not bound by age
Recapture those simple moments at any stage
Remember the child within is always with you
Ready to impart prospective to get you through

No Regrets

Decide what is important to you
Do you best to make it come true

Step back and look around
Are life's joys nowhere to be found

Frolicking with kids on the beach
If the moment is gone it is out of reach

Baby's first step or playing catch ball
If you are not there you miss it all

I am committed from this day on
To treasure and enjoy each new dawn

I do not want to look back and say
I regret a moment of any precious day

The Face In The Mirror

When you look in the mirror what do you see
Can that austere image really be me
The person who stares back at you
Is your harshest critic judging what you do
We present to the world many contrasting sides
But from our inner self we cannot hide
Relax that wrinkled and stress lined brow
Do not dwell on yesterday live in the *now*
Allow yourself latitude and some slack
Show gratitude and give something back
Loosen up broaden the smile on your face
Work on life's challenges at your own pace
Trust in God to be with you all the way
The face in the mirror reflects a good day!

A Difficult Journey

When life's problems over power you
And there's no end no matter what you do

What helps reduce the pain and sorrow
Is believing there will be a better tomorrow

The secret is to feel with all your heart
That it is possible to create a new start

The journey is a long and difficult ride
But knowing God's presence is at your side

Will give you strength to do what must be done
To make tomorrow a happy one

All journeys' start one step at a time
So muster your courage and start the climb

You will stumble and slide along the way
But you will make progress each new day

Cigarette Addiction

Memories bring me back to teenage years
When dating and grades were our big fears

We would sneak off into the pine-scented wood
Covertly smoking as many cigarettes as we could

We laughed and coughed and sputtered and spit
Struggling to puff and keep our cigarettes lit

Who ever thought in those days back when
Those cigarettes would ultimately do us in

It was part of our culture a passage to achieve
Never realizing we were creating a deadly need

How fast the habit takes a strong lethal hold
The monkey on your back is ugly and cold

Tremors increasing needs you try to forget
Your world revolves around the next cigarette

Lately you experienced a nagging dry cough
You huff and puff when you climb to the loft

The diagnostic chest x-ray came back positive
The biopsy will determine whether you die or live

Compulsive Shopper

You walk into a store carefree and innocently
Before you know it you are on a shopping spree
You struggle somewhat helplessly not to give in
But are defeated by the sale persons compelling grin
Your little pangs of guilt and shame are put at bay
Shopping makes you happy and you were sad today
You need that pair of shoes and matching bag
You feel no remorse at the high price tag
You scan the catalog that came in the mail
A handy credit card will complete the sale
You attended the auction out of curiosity
You now own a Louis the Fourteenth vanity
When your spouse pleads do not buy any more
You rant and rave as you slam out the door
Your purchases make you feel in control
For that feeling of power you'd sell your soul
Your new possessions produce a great high
Soon the feeling is gone with a forlorn sigh
Although you may not see the similarity
You're like an alcoholic seeking his whiskey
Similar to an abuser with a drug that is addictive
You need another fix or purchase to feel up lifted
Your home is cluttered from ceiling to floor
With objects that you do not need any more
Ownership does not define who you are
You are truly greater than a boat or a car
If you are willing try this plain and simple test
You will achieve a different high and it's the best
Start by giving away some of your possessions
The act becomes easier with each concession
When you measure your self-worth in terms of giving
You will stand very tall and take pleasure in living

Lifestyles

You cannot live without cell phone, fax and TV
Palm pilot, DVD player, and CD.
A golf and gym membership at a prestigious club
Alas no time to relax and enjoy the hub

Facials and pedicures nail shaping and a perm
Scrubs, rubs and waxing until you squirm
Diamond earrings with matching ring and necklace
Chains, pendants and pearls to adorn your face

The latest digital camera and extra software
That is never handy when a photo op is near
Another new car and a vacation home
Still you fear the emptiness of being alone

Work harder to increase the bottom line
You can boast these objects are all mine
Treasures and gadgets your home overtaken
Not another step for fear of breaking

When did things take control of your life
Do they give comfort dealing with strife
Your house runneth over but not so your cup
Joy is elusive you mourn like a pup

A bolt of lightening out of the blue
Arose the hidden person inside of you
You have forgotten life's simplicity
The fragrance of a flower the sway of a tree

The oceans ebbing and steadfast flow
Watching your children into adults grow
Sunrise sunset season following season
God will show you life's purpose and reason

Where Is The Joy

I own a classy Mercedes purchased new
A sleek convertible in shiny metallic blue
Top down wind blowing in my hair
There was admiration in every stare
It wasn't as much fun as I thought it would be
I think a battery operated Tesla is for me

Nikon just released its latest camera the X23
With options and all extras available to me
A high definition lens and software galore
That will make me happy I do not need more
The lighting is wrong not the best time of day
I'll just box the equipment and store it away

I must have that palatial estate on the hill
I will put in extra work time to pay the bill
It is kind of lonely in this big echoing house
It is boring and lifeless and quiet as a mouse
Where is the fulfillment I thought I would find
Why don't I feel happiness and peace of mind

While sleeping a heavenly vision came to me
I awoke feeling at peace content as could be
As daybreak started its golden ascent at the beach
I was convinced great joy was within my reach
As the sun sparkled on the incoming tide
People hands joined standing side by side

In an instant it became perfectly clear
Fulfillment and joys in life were right here
A generous heart not acquiring material things
Gives great joy and gratitude for what God brings

A Blessed Day

One morning I woke to rain
It wasn't a gentle patter on the pane
It was windswept trembles of thunder

It made me wonder

Another morning I woke to a sunny sky
A cloudless morning…air so dry
I imagined a perfect day

Then I started to pray

I prayed for those who woke in pain
I prayed for those who have no name
I prayed for those with silent voice
I prayed for those who have no choice

I awoke on a special morn
Aware that injustices were gone
Man treated man with dignity

God smiled down on you and me

Conquering Fear

Conquering fear is an exciting thing
A crowning moment you feel like a king

Fear of failure can block and paralyze
Clip your wings and blind your eyes

Hidden in the recesses of your mind
A voice of encouragement you will find

You visualize applause and good-hearted praise
Whooping cheer and voices in triumph raised

Adrenalin pumping your eyes focused on track
You have turned a corner nothing holds you back

I can do it you say with such feeling of conviction
Do not stand in my way courage in an addiction

Crossing the finish line accomplishing your task
Fills you with pride and glory you cannot mask

I met fearfulness and stood my ground
Victorious… my courage I have found!

Freedom To Be

The maiden of yesteryear
Long aproned skirt and plaited hair
Conducts herself with propriety
A stalwart pillar of virtuosity

Hidden from the world to see
Is what she truly longs to be
A lighthearted spirit flying aloft
Romantic dreams and scandalous thought

The girl today with kohl eyes
Studded ears and exposed thighs
Free to explore on a whim or dare
Bold and brave without fear

Hidden from the world to see
Is what peers will not let her be
The young girl deep inside
Is more reserved with concealed pride

This plight has transcended through the years
Due to convention and suppressed fears
If to your own self you are true
Happiness and contentment will follow you

Chapter 11
In Memorium

Barbara Traiger Remembered

The Messenger

Throughout the years since the death of my dear friend Barbara and especially in the early years after her passing I would feel her presence… it's difficult to explain…but I would feel strongly that she wanted me to contact her children. The same circumstances occurred on July 16, 2009. Resulting in reconnecting with her children and now 5 grandchildren. I have stayed in touch and I have been rewarded with watching them grow. I was saddened when I realized her children who were 8 and 5 at the time of her death had a very limited memory of her. I have been the bridge….the messenger…if you will to relay stories and keep her memory alive.

I arrived at your door in urgent need
I think your mother planted the seed

Her lost and forgotten memory
Would soon be imparted to her family

I looked at the man and saw the boy
My heart was instantly filled with joy

I saw her hair, I saw her eyes
I saw her in all your laughs and sighs

I saw her goodness and playfulness too
I saw a little bit of her in all of you

I hope I gave a glimpse of your mother
Who loved her boys like none other

Grandmother Barbara continues her story
Her grandchildren are her greatest glory

The message is she still watches over you
Is aware and proud of everything you do

*In memory of Barbara Portnoy Traiger
whose silent voice is heard*

Everlastng Memory

Barbara, dear friend I honor you
By preserving your memory and just due
Eager and starry eyed
Full of hope….and then you died
You left too soon I know not why
The loss so great many tears to dry
Your story and deeds were left untold
Your children you would never hold
Through the years many and long
Thoughts of you were real and strong
Yesterday is gone; it is in the past
The essence of you will forever last
Sweet sister of my heart and soul
I will keep your memory alive and whole

A loving tribute and promise to my dear friend
Barbara Portnoy Traiger (4/14/42-2/25/75)

Friendship's Eternal Bond

When our paths crossed in the present time
We were drawn together defying reason or rhyme
We smiled and pondered this instant rapport
Are our souls connected as they were before?
We felt the recognition most cannot comprehend
Bonds of time enhanced the true meaning of friend
Our friendship soars unfettered by time or space
Earthly holds prevent not meeting in a future place
So now that you are gone no need for sorrow
Recognition is certain today and tomorrow

Dedicated in loving memory to
Barbara Portnoy Traiger
My friend through Eternity

The Essence Of You

Dearest friend
Immortalized
Forever young
Through my eyes
Called home to soon
A song unsung
Your music lost
To everyone
Your spirit lives
It did not die
It soars of wings
In the sky
Your essence true
Cradles that special
Part of you
Hear the music
Your sweet song
Tears of joy
Goodness carries on

*Dedicated to the children and grandchildren of
Barbara Portnoy Traiger*

Sisters Of The Soul

In loving memory of Barbara Portnoy Traiger
A glimpse of her life and our friendship

Born in April nineteen forty two
Ben and Gertrude welcomed you
You joined Leona, Marilyn to come
Three sister together so much fun
Raised in Chelsea until age thirteen
Mattapan move found me on the scene
You had the gift of leadership
Likeable friendly pleasantly hip
Hadassah, Chasens, class president
A faithful following wherever you went
Our friendship was forged at that time
The depth of which is hard to define
Inseparable like two peas in a pod
So strong a bond did not seem odd
Dances, parties, double dates
Laughing on our roller skates
Entered marriage and parenthood
Hold back time…if we only could
You passed away much too young
More to give; your song unsung
You have a special place in my heart
Sister of the soul we will not part
The gift of you will be told
Your life journey will unfold
My mission is to share your memory
With your loving and beautiful family

The Missing Piece Of Your Heart

Life is a story
An accumulation of
Dreams-Reality-Destiny
A predetermined pathway
Not to journey's end
To eternity

Life is a story we live each day
With ups and downs along the way
We laugh and sing and sometimes cry
Time marches on the years go by
I need to share my friend with you
The mother that you hardly knew
I never forgot her not for a minute
The time is right if you will permit it
For me to impart my cherished memory
Of the person who meant so much to me
We shared our teens and young adult years
Through joys, laughter and sorrowful tears
We planned our futures in youthful innocence
Fates intervention still does not make any sense
Her spirit surrounds us in sweet song
Protectively she watches all day long
She rests now more at eternal peace
Knowing her memory did not cease
I hope that I will play a special part
Finding that missing piece of your heart

Dedicated to Barbara Portnoy Traiger's sons Eric and Richard
and her beautiful grandchildren Shari, Julia, Kayla,
Baila and Asher

Sue And Jill Remembered

The Inimitable Sue T.

She uses her charm….she uses her wit
Her poems are corny and sound like shit

Give up your attempt to write poetry
Stick with sarcasm and prophanity

Putting all joking and amusement aside
Your warmth and caring you cannot hide

You are always steadfast, loving and kind
Friendship's like ours are not easy to find

So continue with your cockamamie schtick
As a friend you are my number one pick

Epilogue:

Sadly Sue passed away on July 1, 2016 after a courageous 8 year struggle with cancer.

Life As A Play

Life is a play performed on God's grand stage
Portraying your energy and spirit at every age
From opening day to final performance
You reach deep for originality and self-assurance
It is the role of your life a challenge to be met
Not a dress rehearsal as you go on the set
Spotlight in place props in the ready
The curtain goes up slow and steady
Improvising tragedy, comedy, farce or drama
Your range extends from joy to trauma
Supporting actors perform with flourish and flare
Whether momentary walk-ons or others more dear
Scene follows scene, acts one, two and three
The backdrop will be transformed accordingly
You have done your best to entertain the crowd
Their response to you has made you proud
You bow to applause and a standing ovation
They appreciate your talent and dedication
Great tributes and rose petals at your feet fall
You will be remembered after the last curtain call

*In tribute and loving memory to
my dear friend, Sue Terrana**

(* Equity player on the stage of life)

A Reflection

In memory of my dear friend, Sue Terrana

I attended my friend's funeral. ….it was surreal!!!

I looked at her casket….it was so cold occupying a lonely place in a room that was too cloying with a scent that had no association with my friend. How could the woman I so admired, my friend, my teacher, my confidant be in that stark box. Unimaginable!!!

The expectation was so great that at any moment the top would flip open and …tah dah dah!!....she'd jump out flamboyantly waving a long brightly colored swath of silk. She really knew how to carry off with flair and style the most outrageous and colorful attire!

But instead that somber box just dominated the spotlight in its starkness and loneliness. Also, carrying with it a message that none of us wants to hear or think about. Like many, I do not like being brought back to this undisputable truth…. But the reality is something we all must face sooner or later….<u>No one lives forever!!</u>

Her message to us is so poignant….. We must do our living while we are alive….live, laugh, love!!

My friend you did just that. The end was tough. Cancer did its nasty job. You accepted the reality with your "tell it like it is attitude". The tears and anger were short lived replaced by your pluckiness and acceptance. You didn't want sad words of sympathy or false hope. You showed courage and in your own inimitable way you gave others, and to me especially, a wonderful memory with your actions, your encouraging words and your unconditional love.

You will never be forgotten. Your uniqueness will live on.

Rest in peace my dear friend until we meet again.

In Memory Of Jill Kabinoff

Jill E's gone!
It can't be true!
Incomprehensible!
What to do?

Vibrant, young......her song unsung
Her music lost to everyone
We gathered by the ocean side
Remembered, laughed and we cried
As I watched the sun descend in the sky
I let you go and waved goodbye
And then I knew as sure as day
That you did not just fade away
Those who had gone before
Welcomed you at heaven's door
Embraced in your father's arm
Shielded from pain and harm
Lessening my own grief
I realized in relief
We will all meet again
We never truly loose a friend

A Sunset Tribute In Memory Of Jill Kabinoff

Farewell dear friend
Your light is not extinguished!
It lives on in the hearts of those who were
enriched by your friendship and love

May you rest in peace Jill

Prayers And Toasts

A Prayer For The Traiger Family

As lifetime milestones come and go
A very dear person wants you to know
As you journey through each new day
Love surrounds you on your way
Embraced in a protective loving arm
Shielding you from pain and harm
Someone special watches over you
With each new dawn you are blessed anew

*A comforting prayer inspired by your beloved
Mother and Grandmother, Barbara Portnoy Traiger,
who passed away so very young but whose
memory lives on in her dear children*

A Mother's Healing Prayer

My daughter
My precious child

I gave you sustenance when I lovingly carried you for
nine months and you gave me inner contentment

Our umbilical connection continues but in a different way

We now give each other strength and encouragement
to face life's difficult challenges

You give me the *will* and strength to overcome an addiction…
and I *will* you to find the resolve to overcome your pain
to stand tall, straight and proud

As we draw strength from each other,
I know each day will slowly bring us to our goals

With God's help and our special bond
we will be triumphant

*I wrote this special prayer at the request of
Donna, a coworker, and her daughter Erin.
They garnered solace, strength and
encouragement from these words.*

A Daughter's Prayer And Expression Of Graditude

God give me the wisdom to understand
that I cannot fix everything

God give me the strength to let go and
realize this is part of an eternal plan

God thank you for allowing me to appreciate
that every moment is special and that
memories are everlasting

God thank you for reminding me what is important
Love, laughter and the giving of oneself

And God thank you for reinforcing my belief that
the essence of the person is never truly gone but
is carried in our hearts forever

*Mom passed away on February 24, 2013
Her gentleness, caring, lovingness,
and understanding are her legacy*

A Comforting Prayer

Proof is not needed…I just know
You are not here but you did not go
You live in my head you live in my heart
Your spirited essence did not depart
You are the breeze blowing in my hair
I feel you saying you will always be near
As you watch protectively from above
My world is filled with wondrous love

*Inspired by my parents who I feel watch over me
and mine and whose "messages" I see and
hear when most needed*

A Remembrance Toast

A toast to anniversaries we celebrate in our heart
To beloved parents cherished from the start
Their wisdom and teachings we draw from each day
And pass to our children in the most loving way
May their love and comfort abound within
May their remembrance and light never dim

IN LOVING MEMORY
To wonderful parents

Ethel & Sam

And

Phil & Eva

Chapter 12
An Empowering Message

Through The Looking Glass

All through my youth and formative years
The lore of the attic drew curiosity and fears

With a childhood couched in caution and timidity
An adventure discovering its wonders held no reality

Even exploring holding on to mother's apron ties
The musty attic held phantoms and prying eyes

Time marches on you leave childhood angst behind
Still confidence and life's meaning I struggle to find

Mother has passed and the old house is mine
Its legend is still etched in that place in time

The emergence of daring to face my own destiny
Had me climbing the attic stairwell breathlessly

I was primed to conquer fear and put it to rest
Knowing my resolve would surely be put to the test

The view from the top of the stairs as I gazed around
Was inviting not dreadful as I thought would be found

The daylight streaming through created a glittering path
To the object of my vexing childhood anxiety and wrath

That full length mirror tarnished and silvered with age
Was the source of my adolescent terror and illogical rage

Bygone images ironically had the mirror beckoning me
Curiosity prevented turning around to escape and flee

As if awaiting my arrival on this momentous day
The mirror showed an assembly of women from away

I pondered the images as far as my eyes could see
The ascension of the generations that came before me

It was like stepping through a time warp into the past
As forbearers revealed the wisdom they had amassed

A resolute warrior protecting hearth and family
She wielded a sword while nurturing a babe at knee

The stalwart pioneer sweat on brow and plow in hand
Worked relentlessly farming and cultivating the land

A suffragette protesting and fighting for equality
Her determination secured the vote for you and me

Remarkable women embodying passion and drive
Doing what was necessary to prevail and survive

They were trailblazers reflecting courage and bravery
Heroines and leaders and survivors of slavery

There were strong women rising year after year
Images of valor and insight I shall always hold dear

Forward looking women who help others to succeed
Inspiring educating and supporting to fulfill a need

Viewing this force of women as far as you could see
Recognizing their powerful bond through eternity

They are the descendants who forged our history
Their significance in our lifetime no longer a mystery

There is a life changing moment of enlightenment
When you discover your voice and empowerment

We are a sisterhood with a bond to defend and inspire
To encourage our strength and light our dynamic fire

Your reflection in the looking glass will bolster you
Your eyes mirror your soul and reflect what you can do

Let curiosity and wonder of adventure negate fear
Be open to worldly messages found everywhere

Find your true self and embrace every possibility
It is your own uniqueness that will set you free

Sometimes it is not easy to be confident and strong
You have the support of others to help you along

As time moves on be ready to take your special place
Joining other women exemplifying wisdom and grace

The silvered mirror shows the next generation to ascend
To be embraced and guided as a cherished friend

Watch over loved ones as your family legend dictates
Encourage through triumphs and also mistakes

This sacred matriarchal heritage will be carried on
In a continuum with each sunset and new dawn

*In loving tribute to those women
who came before and who will follow*

Commentary from Anita Werbner, Educator, and my beloved sister in law:

"Barbara, your poem is so apropos considering the times we are living in. Your poem talks about the remarkable women who had the courage and bravery to come forward to express their desires for a change…like the "me too" movement and the movement to eliminate assault rifles from being sold except to the military and police forces and to update our no sell lists. We need their empowerment to fight for building more mental hospitals and facilities for the mentally challenged. As you said may not only this generation but our next generation be able to carry this legacy of changes forward."

Epilogue

Most of the poems in "Silhouettes of Life" were written after my retirement. I recall that in between period when I dealt with all the elements involved with transitioning from a dynamic career in Health Care to an unknown commodity. The gap between all the challenges and rewards of a high powered profession to the still unanswered vision for tomorrow had been a pressing question. How do I get from here to there? My mind couldn't wrap itself around a new beginning and letting go of a career that extended over thirty years and consumed so much of my awake moments.

I had to explore all possibilities for a new endeavor in this phase of my life. I queried myself repeatedly, in addition to the role of wife and mother and grandmother and daughter, all of which I embraced wholeheartedly with love and appreciation, what would my new identifying label be? How would I fashion the rest of my productive life with balance and fulfillment?

I recall the moment so precisely when this question was answered. It was the summer of 2003 on Cape Cod. I spent hours in solitary reflective walks always drawn to the ocean. While seated on a rocky jetty, arms hugging my knees, staring out at the vast expanse of ocean, I was mesmerized by nature and the wonder in front of me. "How perfect is this creation of God?" I thought. The clouds drifting by, the shimmering ocean, blue gray waters, the birds hovering over their domain, the sand sparkling like minute crystals. All my senses were focused on what I was seeing, feeling, and hearing. I thought to capture this magnificence in words and recall this timeless marvel whenever desired would be amazing. As the jumble of drifting thoughts and unknowns came together and sorted, I saw clearly a future pathway. I could without pressure and with the luxury of time fulfill a hidden yearning to write. As if confirming my momentous decision, a seagull gracefully landed on a nearby wooden piling. I heard squawking and shrilling as he reversed his position and seemed to evaluate and observe all that surrounded him. He paused looking directly at me and for one dramatic moment I could almost hear him say, "Come on, woman, get with it". It was just the prodding I needed. I thought "solitary seagull guarding his post" and then the words just flowed.

My first poem, "Solitary Seagull" came to me in a flash but alas without paper or pencil in hand I was at a loss to write down the words. With renewed vigor I actually chanted the verses in my mind all the way home in a walk so swift it seemed like I flew on wings. I was drawn to the sea daily with each excursion toting paper and pencil viewing God's miracles in appreciation and awe. As if to reward my enthusiasm words describing sights would come with ease and usually with a message to be conveyed. The title "Silhouettes of Life" actually appeared in a daydream. I watched in my mind the words undulating and sparkling with the incoming tide.

I do not feel my situation is unique. We receive messages all the time. The secret is believing in and trusting yourself. Throw cynicism out the window and with an open heart and mind follow your instincts. Let your feet or imagination take you where you should be. "The Old Tree" is proof that when you are ready for the lesson the teacher appears. The teacher in this case not taking on a human form.

So to my dear family and friends and to whoever's hands this book falls into. I hope my words find their way to inspire, give hope, find forgiveness, embrace love, value humor, and open doors to all possibilities.

Barbara Feltquate
Poet

Acknowledgements

To my beloved mother, Ethel, who from the moment of my birth showered me with unconditional love and pride. She made me feel special and reminded me frequently that great things come in small packages. I shared all my poems with her and basked in her praise. I still feel her encouragement as she shines down from above.

To my father, Sam, who taught me by example fairness, honesty, and the meaning of fellowship. He sported a wide toothy smile and had the ability to bring out a smile in others. He truly lived by a code of ethics. His legacy of bursting into song has trickled down to me. My poems show he influenced me more than I realized while in his lifetime and beyond.

To my wonderful husband, Harvey, who thinks I'm amazing and takes great pride in my work. He most definitely changed the course of my life as he challenged me to move from my comfort zone to daring heights.

To my beloved children and grandchildren who light up my life and are my most treasured gift. They are my legacy, inspiration, and source of endless joy.

To my dear sister Janet. As sisters do we are supportive and encouraging to each other in life and in our creative endeavors especially at those times when we question our talent and need validation. One thing for certain we gave our Mom lots of naches (Yiddish word for great pride and joy) as she proudly showed acquaintances Janet's paintings and my poems.

To my surrogate aunt Eileen Kaminsky whom I love dearly and who has lovingly supported me not only in my writing but throughout my life. Yes, she is the only one left who can say "I changed your diaper" and in addition has watched me mature and meet all my life milestones. She loves to read my work and very kindly points out all the typos.

To very special friends who are probably unaware that their support and encouragement over the years was instrumental in giving me the confidence to continue writing and to publish my work. To Toni and Norm (Tatalah) Steinberg, Joan and Bob Goldschmidt and Shirley Pollack and Faye Deutsch. Thank you for your friendship, enthusiasm and earnest declaration that my work needed to be shared.

I would like to posthumously honor two very special women. Lori Josof who opened the door to my creatively, peaked my interest in the possibility that we have lived before, taught me the power of meditation and to be aware of "messages" from far and near. Her favorite expression was "when you are ready for the lesson the teacher appears".

The other very significant person in my life is Barbara Portnoy Traiger. My dear childhood friend who passed too young but who I know is my guardian angel. She is there to protect and guide me and I am her conduit to her children and grandchildren.

Made in the USA
Middletown, DE
26 September 2018